Brock 74   Bible Knox

Some modern faiths

2.

Some modern faiths

Maurice C. Burrell & J. Stafford Wright

Inter-Varsity Press

© INTER-VARSITY PRESS

Inter-Varsity Fellowship
39 Bedford Square
London WC1B 3EY

First edition June 1973
Reprinted March 1974

ISBN 0 85110 368 5

Printed in Great Britain by
Hunt Barnard Printing Ltd.,
Aylesbury, Bucks.

Contents

*The authors recommend that
you read this chapter before
studying any of the individual
faiths discussed in the book.

Preface

In 1956 the Tyndale Press published *Some Modern Religions*, which has met a constant need up to the present time. After seventeen years it was felt that the book was beginning to be dated, and the publishers decided on a thorough revision. As one of the authors is new, it has seemed best to rewrite the whole book, and there is virtually nothing in this edition which is identical in wording with the former book. The slight change of title indicates this.

The change does not mean that the previous book needed extensive correction. Such minor objections as were brought to the notice of the authors by members of the other religions were taken up whenever a new edition came out. But the trend of modern controversy has changed over the years, and it was probably the 'feel' of the previous book that led to a wish for something fresh.

In this book we have tried to present unemotionally the underlying basis of each faith, showing how this differs from Christian belief which is drawn from the Bible. This has meant the dropping of personal criticisms of the founders, except where, as with *The Book of Mormon*, character is relevant in assessing truth. We have kept to the important issues, but the chapters on Jehovah's Witnesses and Mormons are slightly longer, since these are the groups that most people encounter.

We have tried to be scrupulously fair in discussing these other faiths. We have avoided snap answers to views that cut across the biblical position. If, however, we have misrepresented any of the beliefs with which we do not agree, we should like to be told in a letter addressed to either of us through the publishers. We can then make any necessary correction in subsequent editions.

At this point the position from which we write should be stated clearly. Throughout this book we have assumed that in the Bible we have God's true revelation of Himself, and not simply one more record of man's search for God. We have therefore treated the Bible as the touchstone for the faiths that we have discussed. A sceptic might point to the divisions in the churches and say that the Bible can be made to teach anything; indeed these other faiths quote the Bible in support of what they hold. But this misses the point. We are not concerned with peripheral beliefs, but with the fundamental issues of the nature of God and His movement to save fallen mankind.

Our position is that which all the churches, Catholic, Orthodox, and Protestant, including the denominational churches, have always regarded as the truth about the being of God as drawn from Scripture, although some modern scepticism about the final authority of the Bible has naturally affected concepts of God. But the faiths in this book that claim to be based on the Bible have come to birth only in recent times, and hold that the whole Christian church has been in fundamental error in its understanding of the biblical revelation of God for nearly nineteen centuries. The scales must be weighted against such extreme views. They do not ask for reformation, but for a complete rewriting of the Christian faith.

A word about the joint authorship: each chapter was written by one of the authors, and subsequently checked and approved by the other. Readers will notice a difference in the presentation of references, which we ask them to excuse as the personal preferences which authors should be allowed to exercise. We are both most grateful to the readers to whom our publishers submitted our MSS. Their suggestions involved us in extra work, but have certainly increased the usefulness of the book.

Maurice C. Burrell,   *J. Stafford Wright,*
Cheltenham.   *Bristol.*

1   The Faith and the faiths

Please read as an essential part of this book!

EVEN BEFORE he starts on a book of this sort, the reader will have a number of questions which he hopes to find answered. They may concern specific 'faiths', or they may be more general and fundamental questions about the very *raison d'être* of such a book. Before considering the more specific issues, therefore, this chapter will be concerned with the relationship of the Faith, as an orthodox Christian sees it, and the other faiths.

Why is a discussion of these different 'insights' necessary? Surely it is a Christian duty to be tolerant, and, if people want to enjoy some variant religion, why should Christians be jealous? By what right can any religion honestly claim to be the final truth? And anyway, what do you call true Christian religion?

At first sight this book may appear to be making a lot of fuss about nothing. But it has been written in the conviction that religious beliefs are not just optional extras; they are an integral part of any faith. True Christian faith claims to rest on revelation from God, and is vital for that real quality of life which the Bible speaks of as *eternal life*, or sometimes simply as *life*. Other faiths may claim further revelations from God, and, when we encounter them, we shall naturally need to weigh them up fairly.

True Christianity

There are three important aspects of the Christian religion. The first centres in the revelation which God has made of Himself and of His relationship to man. The Christian finds this in the Bible. From the Bible one gathers some understanding of God as personal and as Trinity; of Jesus Christ as God becoming fully man, and dying as the sacrifice for the sins of the world; of His genuine resurrection, His return to the heavenly sphere, and of His future return. These beliefs cannot be proved scientifically, but, taken together, they form a consistent whole, and have brought illumination and new confidence to thousands upon thousands of people.

Secondly, this illumination and hope has not come through the adoption of these truths simply as a system of belief. The system is there, but, if it is true, it can become dynamic only if it is absorbed as a reality to be acted upon. 'Christ Jesus came into the world to save sinners' remains a beautiful theory until I suddenly realize 'That means me'. Then I can see that the fact demands response, and I trust Him as my Saviour. So the New Testament knows two aspects of faith. There is faith in the truth of the facts and their interpretation, and there is personal trust, or committal, to the One who is the centre of these facts.

Thirdly, there is a way of life which follows on these two aspects of faith. In general the Christian naturally aims to be free of the sins for which he has been forgiven through the sacrifice of Jesus Christ. Positively he aims to be inwardly transformed to a life that is after the pattern of Christ's life. He looks for more than merely outward conformity, and for this he finds that the Holy Spirit has come in at a deep level to effect this transformation. The Holy Spirit is God in action. Yet nothing happens mechanically. We are not puppets. In Romans 12:1,2 the Christian is told to present his body as a living sacrifice to God, and, by not adopting world standards of thinking, to be transformed by the renewal of his mind; and many passages in the epistles urge him both to put off the bad and to put on the good (*e.g.* Eph.4:17–32).

It is to the credit of Christianity that so many people identify it with morality. That is one difficulty of a book like this. If one says that So-and-so is not a Christian, the average man thinks that one is accusing him of being bad and immoral. There is no surer way of producing a crop of angry letters in the papers! The point about *Christian* morality is that it is *human* morality. God did not invent a special code for Christians. He made mankind in such a way that 'right' uplifts him and makes him mature, while 'wrong' degrades both the individual and society. Thus through trial and error, through Christian and non-Christian experience, true codes of morals have emerged. These codes provide a sense of fulfilment, and go hand in hand with the aims of Christian morality.

But they go together only for a certain way. Christians do not need to contradict them, but they need to pass beyond them. Thus a code which regards man as no more than a developed animal is obviously incomplete. A code which brings in the aesthetic side will go further, and will make the man-ape see that it is 'right' to throw his banana skin into a litter bin. But until we have the right understanding of man as having a spiritual relationship with God, we still have an unsatisfied and unsatisfying morality.

So we may say that there are three pillars of genuine Christianity, and of these we are treating the first, doctrinal faith, as being of prime importance. By itself it can be dead dogma; one of the sad features of Christianity down the ages is that people have zealously recited and fought for the creeds without ever absorbing them and passing to personal trust in Jesus Christ as Saviour and Lord. On the other hand there have been attempts at inner experiences, Christian or non-Christian, in which revelatory facts have been by-passed, or indeed rejected. These have only the stability of the inner world of the experimenter himself; they are wholly subjective.

Modern mystic and meditational movements are a case in point. Many are drawn from eastern religions, which have developed some useful methods of quietening the mind. Left to themselves as subjective experiences, these methods produce a concept of pantheism, or near-pantheism. That is to say, there is developed a sense of oneness with the life of the universe, which may or may not be equated with a divine force. Christian mysticism, on the other hand, having, as it believes, God's revelation to guide it, enjoys the sense of union with God, but knows that this is not in any sense identity with Him nor the outburst of inner depths of the mind, but that it is the enjoyment of fellowship with God who has shown Himself to be personal.

Doctrines from the Bible

We do not propose to argue here for the Bible as being the true revelation of God. We will say only that Christians have treated it as this from the beginning. We have already indicated that the type of proof that one can offer is that it presents a consistent pattern which makes sense, and that it has opened up the transformation of lives among all strata of society and civilizations. Many would accept this but would want to make a difference between the Jesus of the Bible and the Jesus of the churches; they would maintain that the first faith was simple, but Christian dogmatists have built up a philosophy of Jesus which they have turned into an article of faith. It is important to realize that this is not so.

The Bible is not a book of nicely arranged dogmas, any more than everything in nature is in neat scientific categories. A scientist takes what he finds in nature, and deduces formulae that will make valid starting-points for anyone who wishes to understand the phenomena of the world. Similarly early Christian thinkers worked carefully through the Bible, gathered together the various events, interpretations and statements about God and man, and expressed these in those formulae that we know as the creeds and definitions. Although God has revealed truths about Himself so that we may respond to Him and know Him, and although man is made in the likeness of God so that he can have a sensible understanding such as belongs to person with person, God inevitably surpasses man's comprehension. Thus the formulae about the being of God and the divine-human personality of Jesus Christ were hard to fix, whereas the facts of the virgin birth and the resurrection could be stated quite simply as historical and meaningful events.

The early church records show that there were plenty of ideas about Jesus Christ that were based on one or two texts taken in isolation, just as it is possible to maintain a flat-earth theory by observing a few things and ignoring many more. Serious Christian thinkers were concerned to reach the formulae that would take account of every single statement in Scripture. From their study they concluded that God is personal and one, but that His personal being is expressed in three 'centres'. To amplify this, while we may observe the actions of one 'centre' in, for example, the ministry of the incarnate Son, that 'centre' or Person of the Trinity is not separated from the other 'centres', the Father and the Holy Spirit. No more is the Holy Spirit, whom we now see working in the Christian church, alien from the Father and Jesus Christ. For a fuller account of the doctrine of God as Trinity, which is a major point of attack from heterodox and non-Christian faiths, the reader is referred to the appendix of this book.

Christian thinkers also tried to express the nature of Jesus Christ when He was on earth. Using the language and thought-forms of the day, they concluded that the best summary of the Bible evidence was that in Jesus Christ there were two Natures, divine and human, but He was a single Person. Thus they did justice to the New Testament statements that God became man, and to the fact that Jesus Christ appears as a single Person, not a freak split personality. (An analogy, which the early fathers did not use and which is no more than a pointer to the truth, is that all human beings are genetically two, from father and mother, but certainly are single individuals.)

Christian agreement on doctrines
Now comes an important point. These definitions were accepted by all the mainstream Christian churches, even when they became divided into sections and denominations.

Such minor differences as, for example, whether the Holy Spirit proceeds from the Father and the Son, or from the Father only, are neither here nor there. The significant thing is that, even after the major rift of the Reformation, Protestants and Roman Catholics and the Eastern Orthodox accepted the creeds and definitions as true statements, inasmuch as they could be proved from the Bible.

So, if Christians are attacked for making the Bible say anything they choose, they can say that on the fundamentals of the being of God and the Person and work of Jesus Christ the churches agree that the orthodox creeds and definitions summarize what the Bible says. Many theologians today want to change the definitions, not simply to express them in modern terms, as we have tried to do in this chapter. But in making the changes, they admittedly have to part company with the New Testament as a whole.

In this book we shall be concerned with several sects which profess to accept what the Bible says but hold that the Christian church has been wrong in its formulae. This at once raises a difficult point, because, if they are right, then God has allowed the whole church to be in error over vital matters all down the centuries, until some person in the 19th or 20th century suddenly discovered the truth. If these founders of modern religions agreed on what the Bible says about these vital facts, we might take notice. But in fact they all differ. Hence it is a useful practice for a Christian student to study the evidence for the orthodox formulae, comparing Scripture with Scripture. This is what we have attempted to do in the appendix on the doctrine of the Trinity.

We have already mentioned the obvious fact that there are a number of Christian denominations which disagree over Christian truths. It is perfectly possible to disagree over a number of points, such as the nature of the ministry, the organization of the local church, the significance of the sacraments and the manner of their administration, without losing hold of the great Christian verities. The faiths with which we deal in this book, with the exception of Seventh-Day Adventism, go far beyond this. While the mainstream

Christian churches are making serious efforts to work together, these other faiths have no desire at all to join with others, nor would it be possible to work with them because of their abandonment of the doctrinal grounds on which true Christianity stands.

From time to time one finds that these other faiths hold views which are held at least by some smaller groups of orthodox Christians. Where this is so, we have not gone out of our way to argue against such views, even though we cannot agree with the way in which they are promoted as vital. For example, Calvinism and Arminianism both find a legitimate place among Christians, and we should not criticize a sect for Arminianism unless this has been developed into a doctrine of justification by works. Similarly there is room for varying interpretations of the millennial reign of Christ.

Perhaps the most debatable doctrine which we have refrained from criticizing is that of conditional immortality, held by Jehovah's Witnesses, Christadelphians and Seventh-Day Adventists. This belief is that a human being has no inherent immortality, but that eternal life is the gift of God for those who are to be saved. The lost, according to this view, will cease to exist after the final judgment, and the punishment of this second death will be eternal in the sense that it will never be revoked. Once again, there are many orthodox Christians who hold this view as a legitimate interpretation of scriptural statements. It is not the same as universalism, which says that everyone will ultimately be saved.

These movements accept it in the form of soul sleep, which is equivalent to non-existence between death and the resurrection; i.e. there can be no such being as a bodiless man. Some orthodox Christians also take this view, but others accept a bodiless existence of a person after death, in the traditional manner. After the final judgment they hold that the unsaved will be blotted out.

Finally it may be asked why these deviant faiths arise. The reasons are complex. Obviously they appeal to an inner need of some people, who do not see that this need may be more truly met in the Christian faith. Often the church is at fault. People need authority and need clear truth. If preaching and teaching is at a low ebb and the pulpit is merely a sounding-board for moral platitudes, then the dogmatic agent at the door, with his 'This is what the Bible says', will always capture the hungry sheep. Or if the church becomes more of a business concerned with getting things done and forgets the quiet times of devotion and meditation which answer the deep spiritual needs of men, then the movements that offer inner experiences will flourish. These are two extreme situations; but no amount of examples will explain everything, any more than one can explain why people become atheists. What we can see, however, is that if a person gravitates into one of the faiths, he will choose one of his own type, to fit his own inner world. To take two more extreme cases, it would be quite impossible for a Jehovah's Witness ever to have become a Theosophist.

In studying the faiths described in this book, it will be found that some make use of old ideas which were rejected by the early fathers. Thus Jehovah's Witnesses adopt the idea of Arius in the fourth century that the Son is not God from all eternity, but was the first created being. Christadelphians and Anthroposophists reintroduce something like the early ideas of Adoptionism, that the man, Jesus, was adopted by the Father when the Christ descended on him at his baptism. But many of the ideas are new.

2 Jehovah's Witnesses

JEHOVAH'S WITNESSES are the most missionary-minded of all
the religious sects. Every member of the movement is
regarded as a minister. No-one is admitted to membership
until he is preaching from house to house in an allotted area
and regularly submitting reports of his work to his local
headquarters, the Kingdom Hall. Because of their ardent
zeal in this work, the impact of the Witnesses is out of all
proportion to the movement's size. Although there are only
about 50,000 Jehovah's Witnesses in Great Britain, the
majority of the homes in this country have been visited by
Witnesses.

I have no reason to believe that my own experience is
exceptional, but since moving into my present house eighteen
months ago I have been visited by Jehovah's Witnesses on
three occasions. The last time my visitors were two young
schoolgirls. I have also known a boy of eight to be active in
this work. Every member, from the movement's leader,
Nathan H. Knorr, down to the rawest recruit, is expected to
fulfil his monthly visiting quota. None is exempted. 'Each
congregation of Jehovah's Witnesses is a highly organised
mechanism geared to door-to-door preaching.'[1]

The rank-and-file Jehovah's Witness – the kind who does a
full-time secular job and performs his religious duties in his
spare time – is expected to return a quota of ten hours
visiting a month and to dispose of at least twelve magazines

[1] Notes appear at the end of each chapter.

(*Watchtower* or *Awake*) each week. The more successful members are encouraged to become Pioneers. This is a part-time appointment: the Witness has to support himself on income derived from a part-time job and to spend a hundred hours each month in door-to-door work for the movement. A few go on to become Special Pioneers. This is a full-time appointment; in return for a small living allowance, the member must spend at least 140 hours each month in door-to-door preaching. Last year the average time per week spent by Witnesses in this work was 3 hours 18 minutes each.

The reason for such zealous proselytizing activity is not hard to find in Jehovah's Witness' literature. Like most of the sects, Jehovah's Witnesses believe that they alone possess God's message for the world's salvation. No-one can be saved, therefore, unless he accepts the movement's teaching and becomes a Jehovah's Witness through baptism. As we shall see, their 'gospel' is a travesty of New Testament Christianity. Although the Bible is quoted extensively and many of the phrases of orthodox Christianity are used, what is put forward is heresy.

The word 'heresy' means 'a choice'. Heretics are those who have chosen to follow certain teachings which have been rejected by the Christian church as a whole. Sometimes heretics accept some biblical texts whilst rejecting or ignoring others, and so their 'truths' become partial truths or even truths that have been so distorted that they cease to be true. As we shall see, most of the doctrinal distortions of Jehovah's Witnesses concern the Person of Christ. Before we consider what Jehovah's Witnesses believe, however, we need to recall briefly how the movement began in America about a hundred years ago.

How they began

The history of Jehovah's Witnesses begins with the birth of Charles Taze Russell in Alleghany, Pennsylvania, on 16 February 1852. His parents, who were of Irish and Scottish extraction, owned a haberdashery business and Russell inherited some of their business acumen. They were strict Presbyterian Calvinists and, according to one writer, they taught Charles that before birth God selected men to spend eternity either in heavenly bliss or hellish torment.[2] Russell began to rebel against such teaching, but apparently his Presbyterian background gave him a certain amount of evangelistic zeal for when he was fourteen years old he used to chalk texts on walls where loafers were known to gather.

Then he began to have doubts about his Christianity. He found it difficult to reconcile ideas of a loving God with the kind of preaching he heard about hell fire. Although he changed churches, becoming a Congregationalist, he remained dissatisfied. He turned next to agnosticism and then to the study of oriental religions. He had almost decided to give up religion completely when he heard a sermon by an Adventist preacher named Jonas Wendell which convinced him of the inspiration of the Bible. From that day onwards, Russell was an earnest student of the Bible.

Fired with new enthusiasm, he gathered together a number of friends for Bible study. Their methods were quite simple. One of them would raise a question, they would all discuss it and look up the relevant texts, and then one member would make a written record of the group's findings. This was the beginning of the movement we now know by the name Jehovah's Witnesses. Russell and his followers discovered they could no longer accept some of the basic beliefs of orthodox Christianity, one of the first casualties being the belief in Christ's second coming. When they could find no religious denomination that suited them, Russell (in effect) formed one of his own and soon had followers in America and overseas.

Russell began to publish his interpretations of Scripture in a magazine called *Food For Thinking Christians*, but this was replaced later by the bi-monthly *Watchtower*. The Watch Tower Bible and Tract Society was formed in 1874. Four years earlier small groups of Russellites, as they were quickly dubbed, were meeting in Great Britain. Russell visited this country in 1891, 1903, 1907 and 1910. A branch office was established in London in 1900 and the International Bible Students' Association, an off-shoot of the American Watch Tower Bible and Tract Society, was formed here in 1914. 1914 was the date that Russell put forward as the year when the faithful would be translated to heaven, the wicked destroyed at Armageddon and the world would come to an end. As it happened, Russell's end came first, for he died in 1916.

We shall avoid the temptation of trying to capitalize upon weaknesses of Russell's character. He was involved in one or two lawsuits, including one in which his wife (who had been among his chief supporters) was granted a legal separation on the grounds of mental cruelty. Christians can agree with Jehovah's Witnesses that the movement stands or falls according to its loyalty or disloyalty to the Scriptures. In the eyes of most of his followers, however, Russell was without fault. Some of them said that next to Paul he was the greatest man who ever lived. The *Watchtower* after his death went even further, stating that he did a greater work for Messiah's Kingdom than any other man. Today's Witnesses very rarely read his works or show concern to know about him.

J. F. Rutherford emerged as the movement's second leader. Born on 8 November 1869, he had been the Watch Tower Society's legal counsellor from 1907. A lawyer by profession, he became a judge in the fourteenth judicial district of Missouri. Although he was more direct and outspoken than his predecessor and made enemies within the movement, he proved a better leader than Russell. When he died in 1942 Jehovah's Witnesses were to be found all over the world. It is to Rutherford that the movement owes the name by which it is now known. He named his followers Jehovah's Witnesses in 1931, basing the name on Isaiah 43:10, 'You are my witnesses, says the Lord' (*Watchtower*, 1 October 1931). Before that, members had been known by a variety of names, including Russellites and International Bible Students' Association.

Rutherford was succeeded by Nathan H. Knorr, who has remained president to this day. Under his direction,

Witnesses have been engaged in a large-scale educational campaign. Special schools have been established to teach members how to become more effective propagandists and members spend hours each week equipping themselves for this work. As a result of these efforts membership has increased at a faster rate than ever before, especially in America where the movement claims a 2,000% increase. The world-membership is now about 1,500,000. There are more than 300,000 members in the United States and 77,000 in Western Germany. Great Britain, with its 50,000 Witnesses, has the third largest membership, followed by Canada with 40,000. The circulation of the *Watchtower*, the movement's official mouthpiece, exceeds three millions.

Jehovah's Witnesses describe their worship as 'functional' rather than 'formal'. They observe the 'Memorial' (Holy Communion) once a year, claiming that it should be held on the biblical anniversary of Christ's death, the fourteenth day of the Jewish month Nisan. This Memorial and baptisms are the only 'formal' parts of their worship. The rest consists of the Ministry School for Bible analysis, a Service Meeting for training in door-to-door work and other forms of witnessing, public lectures, and the regular Sunday study of the current issue of *Watchtower*. Perhaps the last is the most significant. Because they all study the same subjects in the same way throughout the world, they are able to speak with one voice on almost any doctrinal issue.

What they believe

Jehovah's Witnesses claim that the doctrines of their movement are derived directly from the Bible. One of their most popular books asks its readers to 'study according to what God Himself has to say in His Own Word' and adds, 'Hence in this book our appeal is to the Bible for truth.'[3] Witnesses are loud in their condemnation of some Christian leaders who have publicly cast doubt upon the trustworthiness of the Scriptures, regarding such action as a further indication that the Christian church is a satanically controlled organization and that all its leaders are of the devil.

Although they claim that their own teaching is simply that of the Bible which they quote extensively, Jehovah's Witnesses often take verses out of context and sometimes appear to be distorting the plain meaning of Scripture to further their own ideas.[4] One flagrant example of this mis-practice is their handling of biblical texts to support their objections to blood transfusions. They maintain that verses like Leviticus 3:17; 7:26–27 and 17:10–14 justify their view that if a person willingly allows himself or his dependants to receive blood transfusions he and they will forfeit everlasting life. In their context, however, these passages have nothing at all to say about blood transfusions but simply set out the Mosaic law banning the drinking of the blood of animals.

Jehovah's Witnesses are prepared to use any version of the Bible, but prefer their own New World Translation. They claim that this translation became necessary because all previous translations had fallen victim to 'the power of human traditionalism'. What they mean is that whereas those who translated the Authorized Version, the Revised Version and subsequent versions allowed their work to be coloured by their own doctrinal presuppositions, the New World translators rendered the truth of God's inspired Word 'as purely and as consistently' as consecrated powers make possible.

Despite such immodest claims, however, the New World Translation is inaccurate in many places and in some places the text appears to have been mistranslated deliberately to support particular doctrinal points. We shall consider some specific examples of such mistranslation as we compare the movement's key doctrines with the teachings of historic Christianity.

One further point needs to be made. Although Watch Tower publications always stress the Society's acceptance of the Bible as the Word of God, individual Jehovah's Witnesses are not encouraged to read the Bible with an open mind and draw their own conclusions, but are expected to believe what the Society's publications tell them to believe. There is no room for disagreement on the smallest points.

This quickly becomes apparent to anyone attempting to discuss the Bible with Jehovah's Witnesses. Every Witness gives the same answer, almost parrot-like, with all the Jehovah's Witness jargon thrown in for good measure. They are like puppets performing the correct antics as the strings are pulled. They do not work or think independently, but simply repeat word for word what they have gleaned from their training sessions. They have, in fact, been indoctrinated. That this is no overstatement of the case can be seen from the writings of ex-Jehovah's Witnesses such as William Schnell[5] and Ted Dencher.[6] Both make it clear that while they were practising Jehovah's Witnesses they were subjected to a form of brain-washing by the Watch Tower Society.

Christ's deity
Christians believe that Jesus Christ is both God and man. The first disciples knew Jesus as a man living and working among men. As time passed, however, they were compelled to see that, although He was truly man, He was not *merely* man. His life, His claims, His miracles and finally the vindication of His resurrection led them to recognize that He was God. Thomas was speaking for them all when he confessed, 'My Lord and my God' (Jn. 20:28). What is more important, Jesus accepted this as a true estimate of His Person. Certainly the writer of the Fourth Gospel had no doubt about Christ's deity: 'When all things began, the Word already was. The Word dwelt with God, and what God was, the Word was' (Jn. 1:1, NEB).

In contrast with this, Jehovah's Witnesses deny Christ's essential deity. Although they are prepared to speak of Him as divine, they refuse to acknowledge that He is God in the full sense of that word. They maintain that whereas Christ is '*a* god' (with a small 'g'), the Father is '*the* God' (with a capital 'G'). Thus Christ becomes a secondary or demi-god, an inferior being.

To maintain this view, Jehovah's Witnesses have to re-translate John 1:1 as follows: 'Originally the Word was, and the Word was with God, and the Word was a god.'[7] There is no justification for such a translation in the original Greek. The text will not allow us to distinguish between the kind of God-hood Christ enjoys and the kind of God-hood the Father has. 'The divinity that belongs to the rest of the Godhead belongs also to Him.'[8] The verse means what Christians have always believed it to mean, that Christ is God in every sense of the word – 'what God was, the Word was.'

Christ's eternity

Because Christians believe in the deity of Christ, they also recognize His eternity. God is eternal, therefore Christ is eternal. There has never been a time when the Son did not exist. Christians affirm that Jesus is the eternal Son of God.

Jehovah's Witnesses disagree. They are ready to say that Christ had an existence prior to His birth at Bethlehem, but because they recognize only the Father (or Jehovah, as they prefer to call Him) as fully God, they do not believe that Jesus has existed eternally. In other words, they believe in His pre-existence but deny His eternity. They maintain that there was a time when Jehovah God was all alone in universal space. Then Jehovah began to create. According to them, His first creative act was His Son. They find biblical evidence for this belief mainly in two verses, Colossians 1:15 where Christ is described as 'the first-born of all creation' and Revelation 3:14 where He is called 'the beginning of God's creation'. We must look at these verses more carefully.

In Colossians 1:15 the Greek for 'first-born' is *prōtotokos*, which can mean 'the first' and 'the chief' as well as 'the first-born'. It certainly does not mean 'the first-created' as Jehovah's Witnesses believe. That meaning would require a different Greek word, *prōtoktistos*. In any case, the context shows clearly that the main point at issue is Christ's superiority over creation, not His relationship to the Father. What Paul means is that Christ is supreme over creation and heir of all things.

Turning to Revelation 3:14, everything depends on what is meant by 'the beginning'. Disagreeing with the Jehovah's Witness claim that it shows that Christ was God's first creative act and that Christ is a creature, Christians believe it means that Christ is *the One through whom the creative work was done*. Christ is described as 'the beginning of God's creation', therefore, because *He began it*. That the words 'the beginning' need not be interpreted in the way Jehovah's Witnesses interpret them is indicated in Revelation 21:6. There God Himself is described as 'the beginning', and not even Jehovah's Witnesses would claim that this means God was the first one to be created!

Colossians 1:15 and Revelation 3:14 support the orthodox Christian view of Christ's eternity, rather than the Jehovah's Witnesses' view of Christ's creatureliness. The New English Bible translators, therefore, were fully justified in translating the two verses, 'His is the primacy over all created things' and He is 'the prime source of all God's creation'.

Christ's incarnation
Christians believe that by a miraculous act of God the Child born to Mary was both God and man (Lk. 1:35; 2:11; Gal. 4:4; *etc.*). He was not only God; He was not merely man; He was a unique Person, who was God and man. So, on the one hand, the writer to the Hebrews could say that Jesus 'in every respect has been tempted as we are' (4:15) because of His humanity, and, on the other hand, Thomas could confess, 'My Lord and my God' (Jn. 20:28) because of Christ's deity.

Jehovah's Witnesses completely repudiate the idea of incarnation, as understood by Christians. They maintain that the life-force of the pre-existent son was transferred from heaven to the womb of the virgin Mary. The result was that Jesus was born as a man, no more and no less. Not content with this rejection of Christian doctrine, they often mis-state the Christian view and then ridicule their own mis-statements of it. Russell, for example, claimed that Christians believed Jesus assumed a human body by a kind of materialization such as that of the angels who appeared to Abraham in Genesis 18:1–2. Rutherford maintained that incarnation involved the belief that Jesus was a spirit-being

27

and that His flesh was merely a covering or house in which this spirit-being lived. A recent Watch Tower book repeats this as 'a spirit person clothed with flesh'.[9]

It cannot be stated too emphatically that these views are not a fair representation of the Christian doctrine of the incarnation. Jehovah's Witnesses are entitled to disagree with the Christian view if they wish, but it is intellectually dishonest for them to misrepresent the Christian view and then condemn Christians for their own misrepresentations.

Christ's death

The cross is central in all Christian thinking about salvation. Christians know that they cannot earn their salvation. They, together with the rest of the human race, are sinners whom Christ died to save. They believe that because Christ died and thus paid sin's penalty, all may be forgiven and restored to fellowship with God. They rejoice in the New Testament assurance that when a person puts his faith in Christ, his sins are forgiven, he is reconciled to God, he is born again and he receives God's gift of eternal life.

Jehovah's Witnesses deny these New Testament truths. Instead, they teach that by His death Christ has simply redeemed us from physical death, and that as we trust Him and work for Him now we are assured of partaking in the resurrection hereafter. That resurrection will be to what they describe as life under favourable conditions. For those who successfully pass through this second probationary period there will be everlasting life – for the favoured few in heaven, and for the vast majority on earth. All this means that, in effect, Jehovah's Witnesses make a person's salvation depend upon what he does for himself rather than upon what Christ has done on his behalf. In short, a person must earn eternal life by his own efforts.

This is a travesty of New Testament teaching. The Christian gospel tells us that Christ has redeemed us not merely from physical death, but from the guilt and power of sin (Rom. 3:23–28; Gal. 1:4; 3:13; 1 Jn. 1:6–10; 3:5). Those who put their trust and confidence in Him are assured here and now of eternal life (Jn. 3:36; 5:24; Rom. 6:23). They are not called upon to work for eternal life under 'favourable conditions' when they have died and been raised, but to accept it as God's free gift here and now. So we read, 'God has given us eternal life, and this life is found in his Son. He who possesses the Son has life indeed; he who does not possess the Son of God has not that life' (1 Jn. 5:11–12, NEB). The New Testament sweeps aside any idea that we can earn our salvation. The only thing we contribute is the sin from which we need to be saved (Eph. 2:8).

Christ's resurrection, ascension and second coming
Jehovah's Witnesses divide Christ's existence into three chronological phases. In a way, each phase is a complete existence in itself.[10] Christ pre-existed in heaven as a spirit being. He was born on earth as a human being. He was raised and ascended as a spirit being. Logically (according to their scheme) though not scripturally, they go on to deny the bodily resurrection of Christ. They say that God miraculously removed and hid the body of Jesus and that Jesus materialized bodies when it suited His purpose to do so. The resurrection appearances, they maintain, were temporary expediencies to support the weak faith of the first disciples. When Christ ascended He ascended without His humanity and is now once again an invisible spirit being.

That being so, Jehovah's Witnesses do not expect a visible return of Christ. They claim that Jesus has already returned invisibly.[11] By twisting and misinterpreting some verses, by ignoring many more and by an incredible juggling with Bible dates, they assert that God's kingdom on earth was established in 1914; that Christ returned to His temple and began to cleanse it in 1918; that every earthquake, famine, war and world catastrophe is a sign of the end, and that there is every indication that the present world will come to an end within the next few years.[12]

In contrast to all this, Christians believe that the risen Christ has a real, though transformed, body (Lk. 24:37–43), that when He ascended He took our humanity with Him and is now in the presence of God 'for us' (Heb. 9:24) and that when He returns in glory 'every eye will see him' (Rev. 1:7).

The Person and work of the Holy Spirit

Jehovah's Witnesses are completely unscriptural in their view of the Holy Spirit. I have pointed out elsewhere, 'As far as one can discover anything about the Spirit from their writings – and there is a significant gap in their theology on this subject – they regard the Spirit simply as an impersonal force. To them the Spirit is "it", and the name is never written in capital letters. The Spirit is "the invisible active force of Almighty God that moves his servants to do his will". '[13] Watch Tower publications state that the Spirit is neither a person nor God.

This view of the Spirit has serious repercussions on their religious life. Jehovah's Witnesses are not noteworthy for displaying the joy which is the Spirit's gift but rather give the impression of being harsh and embittered in their relationships with other people. Rejecting the New Testament view of the Spirit's deity, they do not believe (as do Christians) that every true servant of God has been born again of the Spirit (Jn. 3:5, *etc.*), but limit the number of the *élite* to the 144,000 of Revelation 7. As a result, Witnesses know nothing (and usually give the impression of wanting to know nothing) of either the indwelling Christ or the power of the Spirit. Thus some of the gravest deficiencies of their religion arise directly from their disbelief in the Holy Spirit.

In contrast, Christians believe that the Spirit is not a mere influence or invisible force, but a divine Person. Accepting Christ's teaching at its face value, they believe the Spirit is the One who can teach, bear witness, convict, guide and be grieved, and that in so acting He is demonstrating the characteristics of a divine Person (Jn. 14–16). They accept the New Testament verdict that to lie to the Spirit is the same as lying to God (Acts 5:3–4). Above all, they rejoice in their knowledge that by the work of the Spirit within them they have been born again (Jn. 3).

The Trinity

It will now be obvious that Jehovah's Witnesses completely reject the Christian doctrine of the Trinity. To them, the doctrine is not only unscriptural but satanic. The one God, Jehovah, created a Son, Jesus Christ, and this Son may be called God only in a limited sense and with a small 'g'. There is no such person as the Holy Spirit, holy spirit merely being God's invisible active force at work in the world.

The biblical basis on which Christians base the doctrine of the Trinity is examined in the Appendix. Here we simply note that the grounds on which Jehovah's Witnesses reject that doctrine are very similar to those which led to its rejection by Arius in the fourth century AD. It is not surprising to find, therefore, that Jehovah's Witnesses see in Arius the champion of the true minority view against the erroneous majority view of insincere clerics who, they claim, were perverting the original Christian truth with their man-made and devil-inspired dogmas.[14] The Christian church pronounced Arius a heretic and, more positively, set out the commonly accepted view of Christ in what we now call the Nicene Creed. Jehovah's Witnesses, on the other hand, agree with Arius on every major point.

How they work

Having denied the Trinity, the incarnation, the atonement, the resurrection, the ascension, and the second coming, Jehovah's Witnesses are the declared enemies of the Christian church. They are firmly convinced that they alone are right and that everyone else is wrong. Only they have Jehovah's message for the world's salvation. In their eyes, Christian churches of all denominations are of the devil and all Christian ministers are servants of Satan. This is the background against which we must try to understand their missionary strategy.

Most readers will be familiar with the first step in that strategy, the initial contact, for almost everyone living in this country has been approached by a Jehovah's Witness at some time. The Witness knocks at your door (or confronts you on the street corner), introduces himself as one who would like to talk to you about God, or the Bible, or some recent disaster or current problem. At first he may hide the fact that he is a Jehovah's Witness. Much of what he says at this stage may appear to be harmless. His main aim at this point is to win a hearing and leave a piece of his movement's literature with you.

If you show interest in his message and agree to accept a piece of literature, be it a copy of *Watchtower* or *Awake* or a more substantial book such as *Things in which it is impossible for God to lie*[15], you will be named in his records as an interested person worthy of another visit. This point needs to be underlined. Many people make the mistake of thinking that if they buy a magazine or book the Jehovah's Witness will go away and leave them alone. The surest way of guaranteeing further visits is to accept literature. You are now named in the records submitted regularly to the local headquarters and are marked down for a back-call.

During his second visit, the Jehovah's Witness will be concerned not merely to discuss religion with you and to ascertain your views about the literature he left, but also to persuade you to open your house for a home study group. He will tell you that this is to be an informal Bible study group, and you will be asked to encourage members of your family and other friends to attend it. In reality, such groups are more like indoctrination sessions, for although the Bible is used, texts are taken out of their context in an attempt to show their support of Jehovah's Witness doctrines. There will be little scope for differences of interpretation. Everyone present will be expected to follow the official Jehovah's Witness line as laid down in Watch Tower publications.

If your interest persists, the next step will be to persuade you to join a larger group meeting in your area, consisting of some 'enquirers' like yourself, and some convinced and competent Jehovah's Witnesses like your visitor. Here you will follow a similar course of study as before, but in more detail. The overriding aim all through will be to condition you to think as Jehovah's Witnesses think. Then you will be ready for the next step.

Jehovah's Witnesses do not make the mistake of inviting 'outsiders' to their Kingdom Hall meetings straight away. Only after weeks of the kind of 'pre-evangelism' described above are contacts invited to the local assembly. But once there they are given VIP treatment and every effort is made to integrate them. Those whose interest now persists begin to attend regularly. Every Sunday they meet to study the latest edition of the *Watchtower*. Several evenings in the week they are expected to attend lectures and classes to receive instruction in the movement's doctrine and to learn methods of presenting that doctrine on doorsteps, street corners and in home meetings, for the movement is very thorough in its teaching-practice methods.

It is as people begin to undertake this work of witnessing that they are recognized as one of Jehovah's Witnesses and a publisher of the message. The next step is baptism by immersion. Step by step they have become entangled in the Jehovah's Witness net. They have become Jehovah's Witnesses almost without realizing what they have done.

This is the kind of strategy all Witnesses adopt in their efforts to win converts. The tactics may vary slightly from place to place and from individual to individual, but not much, for Jehovah's Witnesses are expected to keep to a fairly stereotyped pattern in their proselytizing. The effectiveness of their efforts should not be underestimated, however, for they claim to be the fastest growing religion on earth.

How to deal with them

It is difficult to write generally on this subject. Much will depend on the kind of person you are and the extent to which you have a grasp of basic Christian teaching. But here are one or two points which may help.

When the Jehovah's Witness confronts you on his initial visit, his intention will be to preach a three-minute sermon gleaned from the current issue of the *Watchtower*. It may be useless to try to argue with him about this. He has received very careful instruction in every aspect of this subject and, if he has done his homework, will serve up all the *Watchtower* answers. But if you can divert him from this subject, or if you seize your opportunity when he pauses for breath, you may find that he is not nearly so sure of himself on other ground.

He will quote the Bible freely, but do not allow yourself to be drawn into an argument in which texts (usually out of their context) are thrown about between you. Get your Bible, look up the verse he mentions and insist on seeing it in its context. Refuse to move on to other texts until you have done this. You will find that often a Witness uses a text without understanding its meaning at all. Do not fall into the trap of allowing yourself to be linked with any kind of Jehovah's Witness Bible study group, for, as stated earlier, the intention of such groups is to indoctrinate members in Jehovah's Witness teaching, not to study the Bible.

More important than anything else, talk to him about your personal faith in Christ. Show him that your religion is not the satanic thing he has been led to believe it to be, but a living, vital relationship with Christ. This is an experience to which his own movement can never lead him, for it has denied both Christ and the Holy Spirit. Give your personal testimony and pray that God will use it.

Anyone who seriously encounters Jehovah's Witnesses will naturally read two or three of their books in order to see their own presentation of what they believe. A fresh one is produced fairly frequently and the old ones are discarded. In order to get the feel of what it is like to be a member, one should read Ted Dencher's *Why I left Jehovah's Witnesses* or Valerie Tomsett's *Escape from the Watchtower* (published by Marshall, Morgan, and Scott). The second is useful for the average person who is becoming attracted by the movement, since Valerie Tomsett is an ordinary housewife.

Notes

1 Alan Rogerson, *Millions Now Living Will Never Die* (Constable, 1969), p.135.

2 A. H. Macmillan, *Faith on the March*.

3 Anonymous, *Let God Be True*.

4 Readers who wish to study this in more detail should read chapter 5 of Anthony Hoekema's excellent book, *The Four Major Cults* (Paternoster, 1964).

5 William Schnell, *Thirty Years a Watchtower Slave* (Lakeland, 1972).

6 Ted Dencher, *Why I left Jehovah's Witnesses* (Lakeland, 1966).

7 *New World Translation*.

8 R. V. G. Tasker, *John Tyndale Commentary* (Tyndale Press, 1960), p.45.

9 *Things in which it is impossible for God to lie*, p.231.

10 It is doubtful whether Jehovah's Witnesses have thought out the full implications of their view. If, as their own writings maintain, the 'life', 'germ of life', or 'life-force' of the pre-existent *Logos* became the source of the sinless life of the earthly Jesus, surely Jesus becomes more than a human being? Mary supplied his human body without its life. God supplied the supernatural life of the pre-existent Logos to vitalize the body. Jesus becomes, in fact, a human body in which a divine spirit lives, which is the precise point Rutherford argues against in *The Harp of God*, p.103. But this is only one of their difficulties. They trace a connection between the pre-existent Logos and the human Jesus by means of the transference of the life-force of the one to the body of the other. But what connection is there between the earthly Jesus and the exalted Christ who is, according to the Jehovah's Witness view, a spiritual being once more? They maintain that the life of Jesus was offered as a sacrifice at Calvary and that all that there was of the earthly Jesus, including whatever had been transferred from heaven at his conception, was given over as our ransom price. What then was raised? Or to look at the problem in a slightly different way, if the

humanity of Jesus was something he sacrificed at Calvary for ever, should not Jehovah's Witnesses speak of what followed on the first Easter morning as a new act of creation rather than resurrection?

11 They have not always believed this, as W. C. Stevenson shows in his *Year of Doom, 1975* (Hutchinson, 1967).

12 See Stevenson, *ibid.*

13 Maurice Burrell, *Jehovah's Witnesses* (Church Book Room Press, 1963).

14 Maurice Burrell compared Arianism and Jehovah's Witnesses in an article, 'Twentieth Century Arians', in *The Churchman*, Vol. 80, 2, 1966.

15 *Things in which it is impossible for God to lie* has now replaced *Let God Be True* as the movement's handbook of doctrine.

3 Mormonism

MORMONS, otherwise known as members of The Church of
Jesus Christ of Latter-day Saints, do not recognize the final
authority of the Bible in doctrinal matters. Whereas most
Christians believe that God has given His final revelation to
the world in Christ, the incarnate Word, and that this
revelation is contained in the Bible, the written Word,
Mormons believe that God still reveals His will through
prophets. For them, the chief of these prophets is the
American founder of their movement, Joseph Smith.

They believe that Smith's writings, *The Book of Mormon*,
Doctrine and Covenants and *Pearl of Great Price*, are inspired
utterances containing God's truth for His people in these
'latter-days'. Whereas they claim to accept the Bible as the
Word of God in so far as it is translated correctly, they make
no such qualification regarding the chief volume of their
own scriptures, *The Book of Mormon*. One of their leaders
claimed that the manner in which *The Book of Mormon* was
translated ruled out the possibility of any error. This is a
strange claim when it is remembered that some 3,000
changes have been made in the book since it first appeared in
1830.[1]

Although Mormons pay lip-service to the Bible, their real
basis of authority is their own writings. Le Grand Richards,
a leading modern exponent of Mormonism and one of the
movement's twelve apostles, says that it is 'the only Christian
church that does not depend entirely upon the Bible for its

teaching'. He adds, 'If we had no Bible we would still have all the needed direction and information through the revelation of the Lord "to his servants the prophets" in these latter-days.'[2] The implication seems quite clear. *The Book of Mormon* is an absolute necessity for the modern Christian: the Bible is an optional extra. God's revelation to people *today* is in *The Book of Mormon*.

Such a claim raises the fundamental question of authority. Are the Mormon scriptures truly the Word of God (as Mormons claim), or are they the writings of one who was either an impostor or a deluded man (as Christians believe)? Much has been written about the history of the Mormons and there is little need to try to cover this ground yet again.[3] We must, however, take a fairly close look at Smith's visions and the effect they had upon his behaviour, for upon the authenticity of these visions Mormonism stands or falls.

Joseph Smith's own story

Joseph Smith (1805–1844) came from a family popularly regarded as illiterate, drunken, irreligious and superstitious, as Walter Martin clearly demonstrates in *The Maze of Mormonism*.[4] Smith tells his own story in *Pearl of Great Price* and more briefly in the standard introduction to *The Book of Mormon*. In adolescence he says he found himself bewildered by the many denominations and sects claiming people's allegiance. Attracted towards Methodism, he was wondering whether to join this church when, so he claimed, he received his first vision. God the Father and His Son appeared and forbade Smith to join any of the existing Christian denominations on the grounds that all their creeds were an abomination in God's sight. Receiving such a vision, this fourteen-year-old boy felt that a new dispensation had begun and that he had a special role to fulfil in it.

In a second vision which Smith claimed to receive three years later an angelic messenger named Moroni indicated the whereabouts of some gold plates upon which was engraved the history of the early inhabitants of America and the fullness of the everlasting gospel. Smith said he was informed that, although the writing on the plates was in ancient Egyptian hieroglyphics, he would be able to translate them with the aid of the Urim and Thummim, two transparent stones set in silver bows.

According to his account Smith went to the site, the hill Cumorah near Palmyra in New York State, on the following day, found the plates and the 'spectacles' as promised, and started to remove them. He was interrupted by another spectacular supernatural intervention. Moroni re-appeared and told Smith to leave everything in its hiding-place for another four years. Smith claims that four years to the day he returned to the spot, retrieved the plates and the Urim and Thummim, took them home, and began translating.

A man named Martin Harris now comes into the story. Smith wanted him to finance the printing of the book, and gave him a manuscript copy of some of the ancient characters on the plates to take to Professor Charles Anthon, an expert in ancient languages. Smith maintains that Anthon and a certain Mr Mitchell vouched for their authenticity and the accuracy of Smith's translation. Together with Oliver Cowdery and David Whitmer, this same Martin Harris is named in the preface of *The Book of Mormon* as one of the chief witnesses to the book's origin and translation. It is affirmed that these three people saw the plates when an angel came down from heaven and laid them before their eyes.

Another eight men, Christian Whitmer, Joseph Whitmer, Peter Whitmer, John Whitmer, Hiram Page, Joseph Smith senior, Hyrum Smith and Samuel Smith, stated in the same preface that Joseph Smith showed them the plates and even allowed them to handle them.

The translation was completed in due course and named *The Book of Mormon*. On 6 April 1830, when the manuscript was still in the hands of the printers, Joseph Smith and five supporters founded the Church of Jesus Christ of Latter-day Saints at Fayette, New York State.

Although Smith soon had many followers, he was also subjected to much ridicule and active opposition, so he and his followers left New York State for Kirtland, Ohio. He stayed for less than two years, before further opposition led him to move to Missouri and then Illinois, where he and his followers built the city of Nauvoo. It was in Illinois that Smith's career came to an end. Some of his closest friends broke away from the movement because of Smith's alleged immorality and began to expose their former leader in a paper called the *Nauvoo Expositor*. Smith ordered their printing-office to be destroyed and when they appealed to the state governor Smith, his brother and two other Mormons were arrested and remanded in custody to await trial.

The trial never took place. A madly excited mob stormed the prison; the guards made only a half-hearted attempt to repel them, and Smith was murdered.

Brigham Young succeeded Smith and led the Mormons on their historic trek to Utah, where they built their famous Salt Lake City which has been their headquarters ever since. It was not until 1896, after the Mormons agreed reluctantly to prohibit polygamy among their members, that Utah was admitted as a state of the American Union.

In a recent book, Robert Mullen[5] claims that the Mormon church's world-wide membership is now around the three-million mark. Even when we have allowed for the fact that some of these are second- and third-generation Mormons (and may be Mormons in little else but name), it still leaves a considerable number of people who not only believe Joseph Smith's story but are also committed to the task of spreading it and the Mormon gospel throughout the world. Mullen goes on to claim that the movement's 12,000 missionaries make over 180,000 converts a year.

Is it a fairy story?

Was Joseph Smith telling the truth? Or was he a fraud who made up the story for what he could get out of it? Or was he, perhaps, a sadly deluded man who was more to be pitied than blamed? These are some of the questions raised by Smith's account of the origin of *The Book of Mormon*. We must consider the evidence.

The Book of Mormon has more than five hundred pages

written in a style very similar to that of the Authorized Version but without the Bible's interest. A Mormon writer has outlined its contents. 'The prophet Lehi and his family left Jerusalem 600 years before Christ. Under the direction of the Lord they reached the American continent. You can read about this in the first 40 pages of "The Book of Mormon". "The Book of Mormon" will give you an account of these people and their descendants. Within this sacred record you will find the wisdom of the prophets, the experience of nations, and most important of all, a fullness of the Gospel of Jesus Christ. Christ himself appeared to the people of this continent following his death and resurrection in Jerusalem. They were "the other sheep not of this fold" mentioned in John 10:16. When Columbus discovered the American continent it was inhabited by a dark-skinned people whom he called Indians. These people were the benighted remnant of a once mighty civilisation. "The Book of Mormon" explains the origin of the American Indian. It also contains the historical record of a people who lived upon the American continent for a thousand years (600 BC to AD 400). It tells how they prospered as long as they kept the commandment of God; how prophets warned them as they departed from his righteous ways; and of their eventual destruction. "The Book of Mormon" is a timely warning to the people of our day.'[6]

In the light of such tremendous claims and of Joseph Smith's own assertions about *The Book of Mormon's* divine origin, we must now ask whether the available evidence backs up these claims or leaves us with no alternative but to reject them. A number of important questions, therefore, need to be answered.

Where are the plates today?
If they were in existence, they could be submitted to the eye of honest research. Mormons claim that Smith had to return them to Moroni after the translation was complete. To say the least of it, this seems too easy a way out of a very awkward situation.

Does Smith's character inspire confidence?

Jesus Christ made some tremendous claims, but they were authenticated by the life He lived, by the miracles He performed and, most of all, by the vindication of His resurrection. In contrast, Smith does not appear to be the kind of man who inspired trust. He was regarded as a rogue by those who knew him best, and in 1826 when he was 21 he was found guilty of being 'a disorderly person and an impostor'.[7] Fawn Brodie, one of Smith's fairest biographers, writes, 'His reputation before he organised his church was . . . of a likable ne'er-do-well, who was notorious for tall tales and necromantic arts, and who spent his leisure leading a band of idlers in digging for buried treasure.'[8]

Then there is the whole question of polygamy. Smith claimed divine sanction for this practice among his followers, though, as we shall see, the practice has been forbidden in the church for many years. But is a man who commanded his followers to take several wives and who himself set them the example the kind of person to inspire confidence as God's mouthpiece to modern civilization?

What about the expert testimony?

As we have seen, Smith claimed that Professor Charles Anthon of Columbia University vouched for the genuineness of the characters Smith copied from the plates and for the accuracy of his translation. Unfortunately for the Mormons, Anthon's story is rather different. In a letter written to E. D. Howe[9] in 1834, within four years of *The Book of Mormon*'s publication, the professor stated quite categorically, 'The whole story about my having pronounced the Mormonite inscription to be "reformed Egyptian hieroglyphics" is perfectly false.'

He agreed that a man did bring him a paper containing what he described as a 'singular scrawl' copied by a person from a book containing various alphabets. Examining the paper, Anthon thought at first that it was a hoax, but when the man told him about the gold plates and mentioned he had been asked for money to publish the book,

Anthon concluded that it was 'a scheme to cheat the farmer of his money'.

Can we trust the 'three' and the 'eight'?
The three witnesses to the authenticity of *The Book of Mormon* were among Smith's chief supporters in the early days of Mormonism. Like him, they were anxious that the movement should succeed and would be prepared to back up his story. All three later left Mormonism and were branded by their former colleagues as rogues and counterfeiters. Were they any more trustworthy when they were still members of the Mormon church? In any case, their claim that an angel came from heaven and laid the gold plates before their eyes does not mean that they saw the plates as Smith was translating them. In fact they had a vision in the neighbouring woods. As for the eight witnesses, it will not have escaped the reader's attention that four were Whitmers and three were Smiths. The other one married a Whitmer daughter. As a Roman Catholic writer has said, 'It is altogether too close a family circle.'[10]

What archaeological evidence is there for the claims of The Book of Mormon?
Smith claimed that the gold plates contained the history of the ancient inhabitants of America, as well as the fullness of the everlasting gospel. This involves the belief that two great civilizations once existed on the American continent, that millions of people lived there, that many cities existed and that all of this began with the exodus of a small group of people from Israel many years before Christ. According to Martin, 'leading archaeological researchers have not only repudiated the claims of *The Book of Mormon* as to the existence of these civilizations, but have adduced considerable evidence to show the impossibility of the accounts given in the Mormon Bible.' Martin quotes the words of W. Duncan Strong of New York's Columbia University: 'I do not believe that there is a single thing of value concerning the pre-history of the American Indian in *The Book of*

Mormon and I believe the great majority of American archaeologists would agree with me.' He also includes a statement from the Smithsonian Institution in Washington: 'There is no correspondence between archaeological sites and cultures as revealed by scientific investigations and as recorded in the Book of Mormon ... It can be stated definitely that there is no connection between the archaeology of the New World and the subject-matter of the Book of Mormon.'[11]

How do Mormons account for the large sections from the Authorized Version in The Book of Mormon?
The book is supposed to cover the period 600 BC to AD 400. Whoever compiled it, however, appears to have had a copy of the AD 1611 translation of the Bible before him. This seems to be the only satisfactory explanation of the facts. Comparisons of Isaiah 2–14 and 2 Nephi 12–24, Isaiah 48–49 and 2 Nephi 20–21, and Malachi 3–4 and 3 Nephi 24–25 are most revealing in this respect. Many more instances of such 'borrowing' occur throughout *The Book of Mormon*.[12]

Mormons try to avoid the embarrassment of the charge of plagiarism by maintaining that because Smith knew the language of the Authorized Version so well he would naturally translate his new revelation in the language of that version. It has to be remembered, however, that what we are confronted with in *The Book of Mormon* is not occasional AV sounding phrases and verses but whole blocks, sometimes many chapters, of AV material. What may be more significant is the fact that *The Book of Mormon* also contains some of the established inaccuracies of the Authorized Version.[13] However much Mormons try to avoid the conclusion, the facts speak for themselves. Whoever wrote *The Book of Mormon* had the Authorized Version (or a book containing many quotations from it) before him and copied large sections from it. This demolishes the claim that the book in its original form was completed in 400 AD.

Are the claims of The Book of Mormon reasonable?
Is it reasonable to accept the authenticity of a book which

alleges that a detailed Christian theology was being proclaimed as early as the sixth century before Christ? It is true that the writer claims to be setting out this theology prophetically to prepare for Christ's first coming. A more reasonable explanation is that *The Book of Mormon* is a product of the nineteenth century AD. 1 Nephi 11:13ff. and 2 Nephi 2:6ff. require us to believe that whereas the Old Testament writers foresaw the coming of Christ in dark shadows, as early as 600 BC Nephi was given detailed visions in which most of the events of Christ's life shone as brightly as the noon-day sun. Here Nephi is supposed to have become aware of the virgin birth, the divine Sonship of Christ, Christ's baptism by John the baptist, Christ's ministry of teaching, healing and casting out spirits, His fellowship with the twelve apostles, His atoning death on the cross and His resurrection.

The other Mormon Scriptures

Anyone who is dealing seriously with Mormonism should ask to buy these other Scriptures, since they contain some very strange material. The second volume of them is *Doctrine and Covenants*. Sections 1 to 133 claim to be revelations given by God to or through Joseph Smith; section 134 is 'A Declaration of Belief regarding Governments and Laws'; section 135 tells the story of Smith's 'martyrdom' and section 136 contains 'The Word and Will of the Lord, given through President Brigham Young', Smith's successor. Smith's 133 revelations were all received between September 1823 and July 1843. It would appear that whenever Smith wished to guide his followers into some new facet of religious truth, he received a timely revelation giving his words divine authority.

These revelations include the well-known abstinence rule (section 89) instructing Mormons to abstain from tobacco, wine, strong drink and hot drinks (*i.e.* tea and coffee), and to eat meat only in moderation, all of which is still required of good Mormons.

The most far-reaching and controversial revelation,

however, was section 132, dealing with marriage, in which Smith claimed two things. First, he said that whereas ordinary marriage was a covenant that came to an end when one of the partners died, if the partners made a marriage covenant for eternity as well as for time their marriage would survive the separation of death and they would be re-united after the resurrection. Mormons, therefore, have a ceremony called Celestial Marriage, which has to be performed in one of their temples and which, so they claim, is absolutely essential for people who wish to attain to the highest grade of salvation.

Smith's second claim in section 132 was more sensational, for he maintained that God had given him the right to practise polygamy and to enjoin his followers to do the same. There is evidence that Smith and some of his followers had been practising polygamy long before this 'revelation' and that the revelation was proclaimed to justify their actions. Smith's bitterest opponents have always maintained that the revelation was intended to give respectability to the prophet's illicit love-affairs.

Mormon polygamy continued until 24 September 1890 when their president, Wilford Woodruff, issued *The Manifesto* instructing church members 'to refrain from contracting any marriage forbidden by the law of the land'. This was the price the Mormons were required to pay before the United States government would grant statehood to Utah. Since Woodruff's reversal of Smith's command, polygamy has been officially forbidden within the Mormon church and the few found guilty of practising it have been excommunicated.

The polygamy question is still important, however, because of its bearing upon the Mormon view of scripture. As we have seen, Mormons regard *Doctrine and Covenants* as the word of God, and section 132 is still included in modern editions. When it came to the choice of either complying with this revelation and having their property confiscated or obeying the federal government and being granted statehood, however, Mormons chose to go back on Smith and obey the civil authority. This Mormon inconsistency argues strongly against their view that *Doctrine and Covenants* is scripture. If Smith was right, his revelation should have been observed no matter what it cost. Of course, if Smith was wrong, then no problem arises. For obvious reasons, Mormons cannot admit that their founder was in error, for if it could be shown that he was wrong in this 'revelation', who would be able to say when he was right in the others? And if he were proved unreliable in *Doctrine and Covenants*, to what extent could *The Book of Mormon* and *Pearl of Great Price* be trusted?

Pearl of Great Price completes the Mormon trilogy of scriptures. Despite its name, it has little of real value to offer. It contains the Authorized Version of Matthew 24 with a few minor variations, though it is difficult to see the reason for this inclusion. In addition there is an alleged translation from a papyrus which is said to have been discovered in the Egyptian catacombs and which, so Smith claimed, contains the writings of Abraham when he was in Egypt. Until recently it was believed that the manuscript evidence for this part of *Pearl of Great Price* was destroyed in a Chicago museum fire in 1870. According to the *Salt Lake Messenger* for June 1968, however, the papyrus has now come to light. Far from vindicating Smith, it proves he knew no Egyptian and shows that what he regarded as the writings of Abraham are parts of funeral texts from the Egyptian *Book of Breathings*, as *Pearl of Great Price* reproduces a picture from the papyrus, and Egyptologists recognize this as a normal funerary picture with no connection with Abraham.

For obvious reasons we have spent a long time considering the validity of the Mormon scriptures. If Smith's claim to be a true prophet with a message from God for these 'latter-days' turns out to be completely false, then there is little point in concerning ourselves too much with the other doctrines of the church he founded. After examining the evidence against the Mormon claims for *The Book of Mormon*, and after taking a brief look at *Doctrine and Covenants* and *Pearl of Great Price*, we may fairly conclude that whatever else these books may be they are certainly not the inspired Word of God. As we go on now to consider briefly some of the other doctrines of Mormonism, it will be seen that they are a distortion of the teaching of the true Word of God in the Christian Scriptures.

Some Mormon doctrines

God
At the outset of this brief discussion of Mormon beliefs, it must be remembered that, although Mormon writers often use orthodox terminology, the views behind this terminology are far from orthodox. This is particularly true of their view of God. Although they are ready to speak of a threefold God and, on occasions, even of a trinity, they are totally opposed to the Christian view of the Trinity as outlined in the Appendix.

Mormons believe that God is tangible. Arguing from the Genesis statement that man is made in God's image, they maintain that God is like us and must have a physical body of flesh and bones every bit as real as our bodies. They believe that Deuteronomy 4:28 supports this view. Le Grand Richards, for example, maintains that the true God, as contrasted with the idols mentioned in Deuteronomy, can see, hear, eat, and smell, and must, therefore, possess a physical body with the organs enabling Him to do these things.[14] Looking at the verse in its context, however, we can see it demands a very different interpretation, for the whole purpose of this section of Deuteronomy is to forbid the making of idols on the grounds that, when God spoke to Israel, they heard His voice but saw no form. Significantly, Richards does not quote verses 15–18 of the same chapter; 'On the day when the Lord spoke to you out of the fire on Horeb, you saw no figure of any kind; so take good care not to fall into the degrading practice of making figures carved in relief, in the form of a man or a woman, or of an animal on earth or bird that flies in the air, or of any reptile on the ground or fish in the waters under the earth' (NEB). In its context, ignored by Richards and other Mormon writers,

Deuteronomy argues strongly against God's tangibility.

The idea of an evolving God is also an integral part of Mormon theology. They believe that the Supreme God is, as it were, at the top of the ladder, whilst we are beginning to ascend near the bottom. Even God has not always been at the top, they claim, but has climbed up from those rungs on which we now stand. In his funeral address for Elder King Follett (1844) Smith said, 'God himself was once as we are now, and is an exalted man.' Lorenzo Smith made a similar statement which has become a maxim of Mormon doctrine: 'As man is, God once was; as God is, man may become.' Mormon writings abound with this kind of teaching.

Logically, Mormons also believe in a plurality of Gods, for there is, they maintain, a Council of the Gods over whom the Supreme God presides. As well as Jesus Christ, this Council includes Enoch, Elijah, Abraham, Peter, Paul, and many more recent characters including Joseph Smith and Brigham Young. In the funeral address already quoted Joseph Smith told his hearers, 'You have got to learn how to be Gods yourselves . . . the same as all Gods have done before you, namely by going from one small degree to another.' Such teaching leads W. R. Martin to conclude that Mormonism is 'polytheistic to the core'.[15]

Bible readers will not need to be told how unscriptural such views are. They are completely repudiated by such passages as Exodus 20:1–6, and Isaiah 40:12–31 and 45:18, which (along with many others) stress that the Lord God is one, sovereign, and eternal God besides whom there is no other God.

Jesus Christ

The Mormon view of Christ has to be seen against the background of their doctrine of God, where Jesus Christ figures among the other 'gods' of the Council of the Gods. It also has to be interpreted in the light of the Mormon doctrine of the pre-existence of all spirits, for Mormonism holds that our pre-existent spirits were all 'begotten by Heavenly Parents even as Jesus was'. The implications are very serious. Either Christ is a creature like us, or we are part of the Godhead like Him. In both cases the essential uniqueness of Christ, as upheld in the Scriptures, disappears completely. He is no different from us. This means that some of the more orthodox Mormon descriptions of Christ as God, Jehovah, and Eternal are emptied of much of their meaning.

The Holy Spirit

Mormons distinguish between the Holy Ghost, whom they are ready to call 'the third personage of the Godhead', and the Spirit of God or of Christ. They say the Holy Ghost works only in those who have been baptized as Mormons and have received the laying-on of hands of the Mormon priesthood. The Spirit of God (or the Spirit of Christ), on the other hand, is the one who enlightens every man coming into the world irrespective of faith. Mormons further describe the Holy Ghost as a personage who may manifest Himself in the form of a man (1 Nephi 11:11). Although His power and influence may affect anyone, in His actual person, they say, He has a located existence and is therefore confined to a limited space.

There is no scriptural justification for distinguishing between the Holy Ghost and the Spirit of God or of Christ. It is true that in the Bible the Holy Spirit is given various titles such as the Spirit of God, the Spirit of the Lord and the Spirit of Christ, but different titles do not denote different spirits. On the contrary, just as Son of man, Son of God and only begotten Son are all used of the one Lord Jesus Christ, so also the various titles of the Spirit all refer to the third Person of the Godhead. Moreover, the New Testament makes it clear that this one Holy Spirit, because He is God, is present everywhere. In fact, it is His presence within a person that makes that person a Christian and when He dwells within it may truly be said that the Father and the Son also dwell within (Rom. 8:9).

'Not one of our Father's children is born in spiritual darkness,' state the Mormons. 'Little children are alive in Christ even from the foundation of the world.'[16] They go on to assert that our very presence in this world is an indication that in our previous spiritual existence we proved ourselves worthy to be born. Life here on earth, therefore, is a second probationary period. Those who pass this test successfully will progress towards godhood, for, as we have seen, one of Mormonism's chief incentives is expressed in the maxim, 'As man is, God once was; as God is, man may become.'

Christians believe that despite their sin they have been redeemed and saved to the uttermost by virtue of the death and resurrection of Christ (Eph. 2:1-8). They are confident that in Christ they have already passed from death to life and that they have begun to enjoy eternal life as a present possession (Jn. 5:24). In contrast, Mormons believe there are different grades of salvation or exaltation (as they prefer to describe it), and that whereas 'some degree of salvation will come to all who have not forfeited their right to it, exaltation is given only to those who by righteous effort have won a claim to God's merciful liberality'.[17] What this means in reality is that the only people who can hope to reach the highest grade are those who have submitted themselves to every Mormon ordinance. Thus the Mormon way of exaltation becomes faith *plus* baptism by immersion for the remission of sins *plus* the laying-on of hands by a Mormon priest for the gift of the Holy Ghost *plus* celestial marriage in a Mormon temple – and so on!

In places Mormon writers seem to be expressing orthodox Christian views regarding the work of Christ for our salvation. Le Grand Richards, for example, says that Christ 'redeemed us from the fall; he paid the price; he offered himself as a ransom'. A little later, however, he completely repudiates the doctrine of justification by faith alone. As one reads his book carefully, one discovers that what Mormons believe is that Christ died to free us from the consequences of Adam's sin (*i.e.* physical death) leaving us free to work for our own salvation. Richards goes on to state, 'Christ atoned for Adam's sin, leaving us responsible for our own sins. . . . We free ourselves from the consequences of a broken law, and entitle ourselves to the blessings predicated upon obedience to divine law. . . . Hence, as we continue our quest to know and understand the laws of God, and obey them, we increase the measure of our salvation or exaltation'.[18]

Baptism has such an important place in this Mormon scheme of salvation that Mormons are expected to be baptized vicariously for their dead relatives so that they too may be given a chance to be saved. Their concern to promote baptism for the dead accounts for the great interest among Mormons in genealogical research; to this end clergy are constantly being asked by Mormons for permission to make microfilm copies of parish registers.

The Christian view of salvation is very different. Although man was created perfect, he corrupted himself through disobedience and became a fallen creature with a natural bias towards evil. Moreover, man becomes in practice what he is by birth, a sinner; and as a sinner he is subject to God's just wrath and condemnation. God, however, has provided the way out in His Son. Because of what Christ has done by offering Himself on the cross as a ransom for our sin, we can be reconciled to God and can receive God's gift of eternal life. *We* cannot work for it; Christ has earned it for us and we receive it by putting our trust in Him. But when we have received salvation through faith, we go on in the power of God's Spirit to live and work to His praise and glory. We are saved not *through* works but *for* works, as Ephesians 2:8ff. makes quite clear.

The future
Mormons believe there will be a twofold gathering process before Christ returns to the earth to reign for a thousand years, the gathering of the Latter-day Saints in an American Zion and the gathering of the Jews around the Palestinian Jerusalem. During the millennium, Mormons will engage in

a threefold task, building temples, baptizing for the dead and preaching. The preaching will be aimed at those who, though not Mormons, have been considered worthy enough to remain on earth during this period. All who live on during this thousand years will reach the age of a hundred and will then be suddenly changed to immortality. The wicked, though dead physically, will survive spiritually, and will have another chance to repent and cleanse themselves through suffering. Then, when the millennium comes to an end, all will take part in the second resurrection and will be judged. A renewed earth will then become the abode of those found worthy of the highest grade of salvation, the remainder of the human race being housed elsewhere. The damned, that is a third of the spirit world who rebelled before the world was made and a fairly small number of human beings guilty of the worst sins and therefore beyond the possibility of repentance and salvation, will spend eternity in hell.

How Mormons work

The Mormon Church has a great army of more than 12,000 young missionaries who give two years of their life to work full-time wherever their church cares to send them. There can be few readers who have not come into contact with such missionaries, and perhaps been greatly impressed with their sincerity and sacrificial zeal. Mormon literature claims that such missionaries, who do their missionary work at their own expense, make more than 180,000 converts a year in the 51 countries in which they work.

In recent years the Mormon missionary movement in Great Britain has been directed chiefly towards the new housing areas. Here the key to their strategy has been the erection of magnificent chapels which have become the envy of all other religious groups. These buildings act, not only as chapels for informal and friendly services and as schools for the instruction of Mormon members, but also as recreational and cultural centres. They provide a wide range of activities and excellent facilities and serve as bait to attract potential converts.

These excellent buildings are also used as local head-quarters for missionary drives and from them Mormon missionaries proceed in pairs to their door-to-door work in their areas. In an average three-hour session a Mormon pair may knock on as many as eighty doors and contact fifty people. Probably no more than five will be prepared to discuss religion with the missionaries, but perhaps two of these five will wish to know more and will follow the suggestion that they should arrange home-meetings at which Mormon views may be discussed more carefully.

Two other more subtle approaches made recently are the home entertainments evenings and open-air displays. In the first, Mormon missionaries, often without identifying themselves, will offer to provide an evening's entertainment for the family. It is only as the evening draws to its close that the audience is given any indication of the religious motive behind the activity. The open-air displays take place in strategic areas such as shopping precincts or entrances to underground stations. By means of large and artistically produced display-stands the attention of passers-by is focused upon a theme such as that of family life. Once again, the religious affiliation of the 'attendants' may be hidden at first, but once contact is made the Mormons begin their missionary work.

Whatever method is used in missionary work, the main purpose is to convince contacts that whereas the orthodox Christian churches have lost their direction and have forsaken God's way, the Church of Jesus Christ of Latter-day Saints offers a restored gospel given through Joseph Smith which will lead people into the truth. The ultimate aim is to convince people that only within the Mormon church will they find salvation.

How to deal with them

On the whole, Mormon missionaries are not nearly as well-drilled in the doctrines of their movement as are Jehovah's Witnesses in their's. This is especially true of those Mormons who have just begun their two-year stint. They learn as they go along! Because of this, they are sometimes susceptible to a reasoned Christian approach from one who has taken the trouble to think through his Christian position.

We have tried to show that the fundamental difference between Mormons and Christians is that of authority, for Mormons insist that God's fuller revelation has been given to the world through Joseph Smith. As we have seen, there are grave deficiencies in the evidence they provide to support this view. Sometimes Mormon missionaries can be made to think, if the inadequacy of their evidence is pointed out to them. This assumes, of course, that the Christian has taken the trouble to examine the Mormon claims and read some Mormon and non-Mormon literature. *The Book of Mormon* may be borrowed from most public libraries along with Robert Mullen's pro-Mormon historical survey, *The Mormons*. Most libraries also carry that thorough and well-documented life of Smith, *No Man Knows My History*, by Fawn Brodie. *The Maze of Mormonism*, by W. R. Martin, is an excellent evangelical critique of the movement, and Maurice Burrell has provided one of the most recent assessments of Mormonism in *Wide of the Truth*.

In any discussion with Mormons, it is best to concentrate on some of the key issues such as their beliefs about God, Christ and salvation, rather than to get side-tracked on secondary issues such as baptism for the dead, grades of salvation and abstinence from tea, coffee and alcohol. Moreover, in such discussions the Christian is well advised to keep the discussion rooted in biblical material. Little is to be gained by excursions into the additional Mormon scriptures, and as in any case Mormons accept the Bible as God's Word, here is common ground. Try to point out that God would not contradict Himself, so what He says about Himself, His Son, and sin and salvation in the Bible must stand. If the extraneous 'revelations' of Mormonism disagree, so much the worse for them!

It needs to be remembered, however, that the Christian is not aiming to win an argument but to witness for Christ. As in approaches to Jehovah's Witnesses, therefore, personal testimony to Christ is all-important. Tell them what Christ means to you and pray that God will use your witness.

The Reorganised Latter-day Saints

Throughout this chapter we have dealt exclusively with the main body of Mormons, those who operate from Salt Lake City and with whom the reader is most likely to come into contact. There have been schisms within the movement, however, and the Reorganised Church of Jesus Christ of Latter-Day Saints has a following in this country and elsewhere. In some important respects, the Reorganised Mormons differ from the main body.[19] In particular, the Reorganised Church claims that its members are the true successors of Joseph Smith, that Smith never practised polygamy, and that Brigham Young and today's Utah Mormons are apostates.

Notes

1 Professor Anthony Hoekema notes some of these changes in *The Four Major Cults* (Paternoster, 1964), p.84.
2 Le Grand Richards, *A Marvelous Work and a Wonder* (Deseret Book Company, Salt Lake City, 1950), p.1.
3 Readers wishing to look closely at the history should read Fawn M. Brodie's *No Man Knows My History* (Knopf, 1971), or Robert R. Mullen's *The Mormons* (W. H. Allen, 1967).
4 Walter Martin is an American Baptist minister and Director of the Christian Research Institute which has carried out a lot of work on the sects, and is a prolific writer about Mormons, Jehovah's Witnesses, Seventh-Day Adventists, *etc.*
5 Robert R. Mullen, *The Mormons.*
6 *The Book of Mormon and You*, a leaflet used in Mormon missionary work.
7 Fawn M. Brodie, *op. cit.*, p.16.
8 *ibid.*
9 This letter is quoted in full by W. R. Martin in *The Maze of Mormonism* (Zondervan, 1962), p.42.

10 Dr Leslie Rumble in *The Homiletic and Pastoral Review*, December, 1959.
11 W. R. Martin, *op. cit.*, p.46.
12 Readers wishing to look at this question more closely will find it examined in detail in Maurice Burrell's *Wide of the Truth* (Marshall, Morgan and Scott, 1972).
13 *E.g.* in Matthew 6:4,6,8 'openly' is omitted in modern translations though found in the AV, and similarly in Matthew 6:13, the longer ending of the Lord's prayer – but both are quoted in *The Book of Mormon*.
14 Le Grand Richards, *op. cit.*, p.14.
15 W. R. Martin, *op. cit.*, p.81.
16 Le Grand Richards, *op. cit.*, p.100.
17 J. E. Talmage, *Articles of Faith* (Mormon Church, 1908), p.91.
18 Le Grand Richards, *op. cit.*, pp.279ff.
19 See Maurice Burrell, *Wide of the Truth*, Appendix A.

4 Christadelphianism

LIKE MOST of the sects on the perimeter of Christendom, the Christadelphians originated in America during the nineteenth century. Unlike Jehovah's Witnesses, Mormons and Christian Scientists, however, this movement was founded by an Englishman, Dr John Thomas. Thomas, the son of a Congregational minister, was born in Hoxton Square, London, on 12 April 1805. After studying medicine at St Thomas's Hospital, London, and qualifying as an MRCS, he set sail for America in 1832, intending to practise medicine there. Having survived a shipwreck on the way, however, he felt he owed it to God to devote the rest of his life to religion. For a time he continued to practise medicine alongside his religious activities and was awarded an American MD in 1848. Eventually, however, he gave up medicine completely and worked full-time to propagate his religious views, founding the Christadelphians, a title which means 'brother in Christ'.

Thomas had become a keen student of the Bible, especially of the more difficult sections of the prophets and the book of Revelation. He was so sure that his own interpretations were right that he was ready not merely to reject many of the tenets of orthodox Christianity, but also to maintain that only those who accepted his views and became Christadelphians could be saved. In 1834, when still only 29, he began to publish his views in a magazine called *The Apostolic Advocate* and this was followed in 1844 by *The Herald of the*

Future Age. He returned to England in 1848 and stayed for two years, preaching all over the country and writing what was to become a great Christadelphian classic, *Elpis Israel – An Exposition of the Kingdom of God.*

This rather heavy-going book of 450 pages was not very well received at first, but when Thomas made a second brief visit to England in 1862 he found many small groups of Thomasites, as they were first known, meeting in various parts of the country. According to the sociologist, Dr Bryan Wilson,[1] there were now flourishing Christadelphian centres in Birmingham, Nottingham, Aberdeen, Halifax and Edinburgh. At first the movement had no official head-quarters, the members simply meeting for breaking-of-bread ceremonies in each other's houses, but it was not long before Birmingham began to emerge as the most influential centre, and other Christadelphians began to look to it for guidance and for a supply of lecturers. It was during this second visit that Thomas wrote a 2,000-page commentary on the book of Revelation which he called *Eureka* and in which he claimed he had solved problems of interpretation that had baffled biblical scholars for years.

By 1865 Thomas's followers throughout the world numbered about 1,000, the majority of them being found in Great Britain. Growth was steady, if unspectacular, and three years later there were twenty-five Christadelphian assemblies (or ecclesias, as they were called) in England, four in Wales and twelve in Scotland.

One of Thomas's earliest converts was Robert Roberts, who soon secured his position as British leader of the movement by publishing a magazine called *The Ambassador of the Coming Age.* Thomas made his third and final visit to Britain in 1869 and suggested that the magazine should be renamed *The Christadelphian.* When Thomas died on 5 March 1871, just as he was contemplating returning to this country permanently, Roberts took over the complete leadership of the movement and began to disseminate official Christadelphian views through *The Christadelphian,* the method used to propagate orthodox Christadelphianism ever since.

Birmingham is still the headquarters of the main body of Christadelphians, though some splinter groups look elsewhere for their doctrinal leads.[2]

Roberts, developing many of Thomas's embryonic ideas, wrote a detailed treatment of his views in *Christendom Astray*, a book which was intended, as its title makes clear, to demonstrate the wide gulf between Christadelphian and orthodox Christian teachings. It has been reprinted many times as a standard textbook. Throughout the book, Roberts emphasized that whereas Christianity, as represented by the churches of the various denominations, had turned its back on the Bible, Christadelphianism had based its views entirely upon the Scriptures.

The Christadelphians are essentially a lay movement and there are no professional clergy or ministers. Local ecclesias are run by male members and a very high proportion of the movement's membership takes a full part in its activities. Regular meetings include a weekly breaking-of-bread ceremony, a Sunday evening lecture intended for the public at large, a weekly Bible class and a women's meeting. Evangelistic work of a rather sober kind is intellectual in tone and is carried out through public lectures, personal contacts, well-organized and well-publicized Bible exhibitions, and attractive literature.

There are probably about 25,000 Christadelphians in Great Britain and fewer than that number in the rest of the world. They are one of the smaller sects, therefore, as Mormons, Jehovah's Witnesses and Christian Science have memberships that run into millions. Christadelphians are sometimes confused with Jehovah's Witnesses and in some respects their teachings are very similar. At the end of this chapter, therefore, these teachings will be compared.

What they believe

The Bible
Like their founder, Christadelphians recognize the supreme authority of the Bible. As well as attending a weekly Bible

class, members follow a carefully planned course of daily
Bible readings. Like evangelical Christians, they claim to
base their belief and their practice on the teachings of the
Scriptures. Nevertheless, they have rejected some of the most
basic Christian doctrines, doctrines which Christians believe
are derived directly from the Bible.

God

The Christian view of God as Trinity is outlined in the
Appendix. We have tried to show from the Scriptures that
the only view of God that does justice to all the facts stated
in the Bible is that which, whilst acknowledging that there is
one God, nevertheless recognizes that the Godhead consists
of Father, Son and Holy Spirit who are, in the words of the
Athanasian Creed, 'co-equal and co-eternal'.

This view is rejected by Christadelphians. Thomas's view
(given in some detail in *Elpis Israel* and in an even more
speculative book, *Phanerosis*, which has proved something of
an embarrassment to some modern intelligent Christadelphians) may be summarized as follows. There is only one
being, the Eternal God, whose deity is underived and who is
originally immortal in every sense. Below Him, however, are
a whole host of Elohim or gods who were created by Him
before the world was made and who were put to the test by
Him in another sphere. As a result of this successful period of
probation, during which they existed as mortal men, these
Elohim have now been raised to the status of immortal and
incorruptible beings. They are, in effect, secondary gods.
Similarly, it is possible for today's humans to become
tomorrow's Elohim. Jesus has already lead the way, for
though once a man he has now been raised to the nature of
the Elohim.

Roberts' teaching about God was much more cautious
than Thomas's and, although he did follow some of his
leader's ideas, his main concern was not to speculate about
the Elohim but to attack the Christian view of the Trinity.
He said, 'Trinitarianism propounds – not a mystery, but a
contradiction – a stultification – an impossibility.'[3] How, he

asked, could God be called Father unless He preceded and brought into existence the Son? Developing another of Thomas's themes, Roberts tried to discredit the Christian view that God is spirit, that He is without body or parts. His own view was that God has a physical body with all its organs, 'that the Father is a tangible person'.[4]

Although present-day Christadelphians are as opposed to the doctrine of the Trinity as Thomas and Roberts were, they appear to be divided in their attitude to the earlier Christadelphian views about secondary gods. A previous editor of *The Christadelphian* told me, 'Generally Dr Thomas's teaching on the Elohim in *Elpis Israel* is accepted,' though he qualified this by adding that an accurate summary of the Christadelphian view is that 'there is one Eternal God, the supreme, and there are beings of angelic rank who possess immortality, but as to how and when they attained that immortality the Scriptures are silent'.[5] On the other hand, another Christadelphian writer is prepared to deny categorically Thomas's speculations and to affirm, 'He is not the supreme God among many Gods but the only God.'[6] The same writer told me, 'So far as I am able to follow Dr Thomas's arguments, I cannot say that I find them altogether convincing . . . and I am not alone in this.'[7]

Readers may be interested to see the similarities at certain points between the Christadelphian view of God outlined above and the Mormon view of God examined in chapter 3.

Jesus Christ
The Bible teaches that the Father sent His Son, who from all eternity has shared with Him the glory of the Godhead, to be the Saviour of the world. This is part of what is involved in believing in the Trinity. Rejecting the Trinity, Christadelphians therefore take issue with Christians on three points concerning the Person of Christ, His deity, His eternity and His incarnation.

Because they believe that the Father alone is God in the full sense, Christadelphians are compelled to reject Christ's deity. This means that, although they are prepared to speak of Him as divine, they regard His divinity as of a derived and secondary kind. To them, therefore, Christ occupies a position similar to that of the other Elohim, for, in Thomas's terms, He is just one of the numerous Elohim created by the supreme God who, by their previous human lives of faith and obedience, have earned the right to be raised to the divine status. This is far removed from the Bible's teaching about the Person of Christ in such verses as John 1:1 and Hebrews 1:1–9.

Christadelphians maintain, 'The Son only came into existence when the virgin Mary gave birth to Jesus.'[8] In other words, they reject not only Christ's eternity, but also His pre-existence. We saw in the chapter about Jehovah's Witnesses that members of that movement, following the ancient Arian heresy, claim that the Son of God was not eternal but came into existence at a distinct point in time. Nevertheless Jehovah's Witnesses do recognize the Son's pre-existence. Christadelphians go further than Arians and Jehovah's Witnesses, maintaining that before the first Christmas day the Son had no existence at all, except as a thought in the mind of God.

Readers familiar with the Bible will recall the great pre-existence passages of John's Gospel. The author, claiming to be a faithful witness to Christ, records Him saying, 'I am that living bread which has come down from heaven' (6:51, NEB), 'God is the source of my being, and from him I come. I have not come of my own accord; he sent me' (8:42), 'Before Abraham was born, I am' (8:58), 'I came from the Father and have come into the world. Now I am leaving the world again and going to the Father' (16:28), and 'Father, glorify me in thine own presence with the glory which I had with thee before the world began' (17:5). Radical theologians get round the implication of such verses by stating that the author is simply putting into the mouth of Jesus what the first-century church had come to believe about Him. Christadelphians, though they claim to accept the Scriptures at their face value, take an even less convincing way out. These verses, we are asked to believe, indicate no more than the fact that the Son existed as a purpose in the divine will. Taking them as they stand, however, these verses indicate at the very least that Jesus was conscious of His personal pre-existence with the Father.

It is a short but inevitable step from the denial of Christ's deity and eternity to the rejection of His incarnation. If He is not God in the full personal sense, and if He did not exist before He was born of the Virgin Mary, then obviously it is nonsense to speak of His *becoming* man in the sense understood by Christians. God did not become man. Moreover, Jesus did not become the Christ until He was baptized. Thereafter, all through His earthly life, say Christadelphians, He remained man. It was not until He was raised from the dead that His humanity was transformed into divinity. Contrary to what orthodox Christians believe, therefore, Christadelphians will not agree that Jesus Christ ascended into heaven as the God-man, though they do say 'he is now the corporealisation of life-spirit as it exists in the Deity', whatever that means!

Readers familiar with the history of Christian doctrine will not need to be reminded that these views of Christ's Person were current in the second, third and fourth centuries AD. Christadelphianism is a modern form of adoptionism.[9] Now, as then, adoptionism is rejected by the Christian church as a travesty of New Testament teaching.

The Holy Spirit
As we saw in chapter 2, Christians believe that the Holy Spirit is not a mere influence or invisible force, but a divine Person, the third Person of the Trinity. Christians believe that such a view of the Spirit's Person is necessary to do justice to the New Testament's teaching, especially in John 14 to 16.

Christadelphians deny the personality of the Spirit but admit His eternity. This is quite logical in their doctrinal system for to them the Spirit is 'an unseen power emanating from the Deity, filling all space, and by which He is everywhere present. . . . It is the medium by which He upholds the whole creation'.[10] Christadelphians affirm that it was this power that enabled the apostles to perform miracles but claim that it does not dwell in believers today or they would be able to perform similar miracles. So Roberts states, 'There is no manifestation of the Spirit in these days. The power of continuing the manifestation doubtless died with the apostles.'[11] As we shall see, this has repercussions for the movement's doctrine of salvation, for unlike Christians Christadelphians do not believe that people are converted to Christ as they respond to the Holy Spirit at work within them.

Salvation

'Nothing will save a man in the end but an exact knowledge of the will of God as contained in the Scriptures, and faithful carrying out of the same,' wrote Roberts.[12] Against this, we are justified in asking, 'Who then can be saved?' The greatest biblical scholar would not claim 'an exact knowledge of the will of God as contained in the Scriptures'. The godliest saint would not dare to affirm that he has faithfully carried out 'the same'. Even allowing for a certain amount of hyperbole in Roberts' statement, it does indicate the direction his thoughts were taking. Salvation, he felt, resulted from the combination of an intellectual grasp of the Bible's teaching and a life of good works.

To this day, Christadelphians remain strongly opposed to the doctrine of justification by faith alone, considering it to be one of Christianity's corruptions. For them real faith is not faith in a person, the Christ of whom the biblical Thomas could say, 'My Lord and my God', but mental assent to Christadelphian doctrines, the reception of Christadelphian baptism that goes with it, and a good life. That this is no exaggeration of their position will be seen from their view that infants and imbeciles cannot be saved, for both are incapable of indulging in this kind of intellectual exercise.

All of this is closely tied up with the Christadelphian belief that man has no inherent immortality. When animal man dies, Christadelphians believe, everything that there is of him perishes. His only hope for the future lies in resurrection. Therefore, those incapable of response (like infants and the insane) or found unworthy (through wickedness or a deliberate refusal to respond to God's Word) will not be raised.

It is not surprising to find, in view of all this, that Christadelphianism provides its adherents with no assurance of salvation. After all, if salvation depends upon what I do, rather than on what Christ has done, who may tell whether I have done enough to earn God's approval? Even baptism, though regarded as indispensable to salvation, can do nothing more than make the Christadelphian 'a lawful candidate for that "birth of the spirit" from the grave, which will finally constitute him a "son of God, being of the children of the resurrection".... His ultimate acceptance will depend upon the character he develops in this new relation'.[13]

How, then, are we to interpret what Christ did on the cross? The Christadelphian view is that the cross was simply a declaration of God's righteousness. Roberts sets the view out clearly in his book *The Blood of Christ* and uses Romans 3:21–25 to try to prove it. No student of the New Testament will wish to argue that this is not *one* aspect of the meaning of the cross, but for Roberts and modern Christadelphians it would appear to be its only meaning. Certainly, they will have nothing to do with any idea that Christ died instead of us or that He paid the price of our sin, although both are clearly taught in Scripture (Rom. 5:6–8; 1 Cor. 15:3; Gal. 2:20; 3:13, *etc.*). In their view, God forgives us simply on the basis of His forbearance, if we acknowledge His righteousness and turn to Him in repentance and obedience.

The kingdom

Teaching about the cross is far less prominent in Christadelphian literature than is teaching about the kingdom. When Christadelphians speak about the kingdom, however, they have in mind their own particular interpretation of prophecy. Briefly, their view is as follows. The promise made to Abraham concerning the land of Canaan will be fulfilled literally at some future date. Then the Jews will be gathered in Palestine, the ancient kingdom of Israel will be restored, and Jesus will return to reign on earth. A new Temple will be erected and sacrifices will again be offered. All the faithful will be raised and given immortality, but the wicked will be annihilated.

This emphasis of the kingdom on earth arises out of the Christadelphian view of heaven. Heaven is regarded as the abode of God, but human beings do not go there at death or at any subsequent time. When Paul says that death is departure to be with the Lord (Phil. 1:23), he is thought to refer to the time when the Lord returns to earth at the resurrection. Yet in 1 Thessalonians 4:14 Paul says 'by the word of the Lord' that when Jesus returns 'God will bring *with him* those who have fallen asleep'. The straightforward interpretation of this is in the light of Christ's assurance that He was returning to His Father's house to prepare a place for His people (Jn. 14:2). Naturally, also, the Christadelphian view of departure to be with Christ is governed by their belief in soul sleep, which is equivalent to non-existence, between death and resurrection (see chapter 1).

Christadelphians and Jehovah's Witnesses
Because of certain close doctrinal affinities between the two movements, Christadelphians and Jehovah's Witnesses are sometimes confused. It may be helpful, therefore, to notice some of the main similarities and differences.

The two movements agree that only one Being and one Person may be called God in the full sense, and that all other divinity is derived divinity. It follows that both are unequivocal in their denial of the doctrine of the Trinity, regarding it at best as a misinterpretation of Scripture and at worst as a modern version of Greek mythology or a complete fabrication inspired by Satan. There is no place in either movement, therefore, for the orthodox Christian view that Christ is both God and man, and that He is the eternal Son of God. Similarly, the Christian view that the Holy Spirit is the third Person of the Trinity is rejected by both.

There are, however, some differences in their beliefs about

67

Christ. Both agree that He has not existed from all eternity with the Father, but that He came into existence at a distinct point in time through a creative act of God. But whereas Jehovah's Witnesses think of the Son as God's first creative act and believe in Christ's pre-existence, Christadelphians deny His pre-existence as well as His eternity, and say that He did not exist in any personal sense before He was born of Mary.

Both movements follow the traditional view that Christ's atonement was made necessary by Adam's fall in the garden of Eden, but they limit what was lost by Adam's transgression to ordinary physical life. They agree, therefore, in rejecting belief in the immortality of the soul as an unscriptural doctrine, pagan in origin. They agree, also, that the wicked will be annihilated. For both movements, eternal life will mean a kind of physical life immortalized as a result of Christ's resurrection.

There are marked differences between the two movements' views of the nature of the atonement. Whereas the whole Jehovah's Witness concept revolves around the word 'ransom', with the view that Christ as a perfect human being became the ransom to divine justice, Christadelphians practically ignore the word 'ransom' and see the key-thought of the atonement as a declaration of God's righteousness.

Both reject the biblical concept of justification by faith and replace it with a system of salvation by human achievement.

Notes

1 Bryan Wilson, *Sects and Society* (Heinemann, 1961), written by a leading British sociologist, contains the fullest recent investigation of Christadelphianism.
2 In this country the principal schismatic wings have effected a reunion (Bryan Wilson, *Religious Sects* (World University Library, 1970), p.109).
3 R. Roberts, *Christendom Astray* (The Dawn Book Supply, 1958), p.77.

4 R. Roberts, *op. cit.*, p.79.

5 John Carter, in a letter to Maurice Burrell, 21 November 1961.

6 E. J. Newman, *The God Whom We Worship*.

7 Letter to Maurice Burrell, 20 March 1962.

8 J. J. Andrew, *The Real Christ* (The Dawn Book Supply, 1948), p.71.

9 Bishop Wand has described (in *The Four Great Heresies* (Mowbrays, 1967), pp.23ff.) how the author of the Fourth Gospel found himself fighting on two fronts. On the one hand were those people who were not convinced that Jesus was divine in the full sense, and on the other hand were those who were not convinced that He was really human. Whereas the first group tended to think of Jesus as a mere man, the others thought of Him as a divine apparition. Wand goes on to show how the two extremes persisted throughout the early history of the church, resulting in the adoptionist heresies on the one hand and pneumatic heresies on the other. Christadelphians are a modern version of adoptionism, for they hold that Jesus is not God in the full sense but has been raised by God to some kind of divine status.

10 J. J. Andrew, *op. cit.*, pp.65f.

11 R. Roberts, *op. cit.*, p.86.

12 R. Roberts, *op. cit.*, pp.57ff.

13 R. Roberts, *op. cit.*, pp.236f.

5 Christian Science

THE FOUNDER of Christian Science was Mrs Mary Baker Eddy (1821–1910). Baker was the family name, and her parents were strict New England Calvinists. In her teens Mary began to pull away from her Puritan background, and embarked on a search for other religious patterns. In 1843 she married her first husband, George Glover, but she was widowed within a year. A child, George, was born shortly afterwards, but, because of certain domestic difficulties, at about the age of seven he was unofficially adopted by a friend's family living at some distance from the Glover home, and mother and son drifted apart.

In 1853 she married Daniel Patterson, a dentist, but this marriage was a failure, Patterson turning out to be an unstable character. Mary obtained a divorce for desertion in 1873. Meanwhile in 1870 she began courses of lectures in healing. In 1877 she married Asa Gilbert Eddy, who had been one of her students and who had become a Christian Science practitioner. He died in 1882, and Mrs Eddy announced that he had been 'mentally assassinated' by one of her rebellious students. The fear of malicious mental attacks on herself remained with her for most of her life.

While her ideas were forming, she came under the influence of a healer named Phineas Quimby. He began as a mesmerist, or hypnotist, and gradually came to realize the power of mind over matter even when patients were not hypnotized. We cannot here discuss the influence of Quimby on Mrs Eddy, or, as Christian Scientists think, the influence of Mrs Eddy on Quimby, but practitioners of mind cure are bound to have certain assumptions in common.

Quimby had just died when in 1866 Mary (Patterson) had a serious fall on an icy pavement. The medical evidence of her case is dubious, but she herself claimed that at this time the basic principles of healing were revealed to her, and she was instantly cured. From this time onwards she developed the ideas which ultimately were incorporated in her textbook. The ideas crystallized as she taught pupils her system of healing.

The first draft of her book, *Science and Health with Key to the Scriptures*, appeared in 1875, and, after various revisions and additions, it was standardized in 1907, so that now all editions, whatever the size of the type, have identical paging. All references in this chapter are to pages in this book unless some other title is given. Before her death Mrs Eddy was able to secure by law that at any Christian Science service only the Bible and *Science and Health* might be read, without any preaching or exposition. This secures absolute uniformity among the churches, and eliminates private interpretations or deviations by ministers. The ruling does not exclude public lectures by authorized speakers.

Thus Christian Science, like Mormonism, accepts two inspired books, one of them the Bible. 'As adherents of Truth, we take the inspired Word of the Bible as our sufficient guide to eternal life' (p.497). Naturally the Bible is read in the light of the newer 'scripture'. Mrs Eddy wrote in *Miscellany* that, while she could not write the book after sunset, at the rising of the sun 'the influx of divine interpretations would pour in upon my spiritual sense as gloriously as the sunlight on the material senses. It was not myself, but the divine power of Truth and Love, infinitely above me, which dictated *Science and Health with Key to the Scriptures*. . . . I should blush to write of the book as I have, were it of human origin, and were I, apart from God, its author. But, as I was only a scribe echoing the harmonies of heaven in divine metaphysics, I cannot be super-modest in my estimate of the Christian Science textbook' (pp.114–115).

In spite of these high claims, the book is in its own way as tortuous to read as *The Book of Mormon*. Although its various subjects are divided into chapters, these are muddled and repetitive. It is only gradually that one picks up Mrs Eddy's underlying philosophy, and single sentences may be misleading if they are quoted in isolation. What is said in one place may be contradicted or modified elsewhere. Thus on page 411 we find, 'The procuring cause and foundation of all sickness is fear, ignorance, or sin', but on page 419, 'Neither disease itself, sin, nor fear, has the power to cause disease.'

Healings
Before discussing the philosophy of the book, we may look at the claims for healing, since these are what the average person regards as Christian Science. Although the book contains testimonies of healings in chapter xviii, we cannot check them against medical records. Other cases are quoted in *The Continuing Spirit* by Norman Beasley. Many of the cures could be classified as psychosomatic, as indeed many orthodox Christian healings can be. Few are impressive, but Charles Braden in *Christian Science Today* refers to Mrs David Oliver of Chicago who was 'the first instance recorded of recovery from generalized blastomycosis' (p.252). This is a fungus affection of the respiratory tract, which nowadays is treated with one of the sulfa drugs. Mrs Oliver turned to Christian Science after being given up by the doctors. On the other hand Braden records that on occasions Christian Scientist practitioners have been prosecuted when their patients died through, it is alleged, lack of proper medical aid. A practitioner, Margaret Laird, was struck off the Christian Science register in 1948 because she had assented to the use of medical aid for some of her patients.

Naturally one looks for a proper medical report before and after the healing, such as the Roman Catholic investigators have before them in pronouncing on cures at Lourdes. But Mrs Eddy turns the desire for evidence by saying that 'a physical diagnosis of disease – since mortal mind must be the cause of disease – tends to induce disease' (p.370). For this reason the movement is against Christian Scientists becoming nurses in general hospitals, and dislikes health instruction for children in schools. In earlier days healing testimonies in the journals were said to have been authenticated. Nowadays they are said to have been carefully verified 'to the best of our ability'. This verification means that the healing is attested by two church members, not necessarily doctors.

Although Christian Scientists normally avoid doctors, on the ground that their attitude to disease as real induces wrong thinking about it, they often appear to the outsider to be hopelessly inconsistent. Mrs Eddy herself wore glasses and dentures, and received morphine injections to relieve pain from a stone in the kidney. She allows for this as follows: 'If from an injury or from any cause, a Christian Scientist were seized with pain so violent that he could not treat himself mentally – and the Scientists had failed to relieve him – the sufferer could call a surgeon, who would give him a hypodermic injection; then, when the belief of pain was lulled, he could handle his own case mentally. Thus it is that we "prove all things; (and) hold fast that which is good" ' (p.464). Again, 'Until the advancing age admits the efficacy and supremacy of Mind, it is better for Christian Scientists to leave surgery and the adjustment of broken bones and dislocations to the fingers of a surgeon, while the mental healer confines himself chiefly to mental reconstruction and to the prevention of inflammation' (p.401).

If, like some Christian writers, Mrs Eddy had been content to speak of the power of positive thinking as part of the divine plan for the health of body and mind, she would have contributed something of value to the Christian church. But she dissociates her methods from all other forms of spiritual healing. The technical difference between herself and others is that, while a faith-healer asserts that God is able to cure the disease, which really exists, the Christian Science practitioner declares that the apparent disease has no real existence.

73

Christian Science as a philosophy

This brings us to the strange philosophical system to which the healings are linked. Basically the whole system rests on the assertion that spirit and matter are wholly incompatible. 'Spirit never created matter' (p.335). 'Matter has no life to lose, and Spirit never dies. . . . This shows that matter did not originate in God, Spirit, and is not eternal' (p.275). A Christian would comment that there is no necessary inconsistency in holding that matter originated in God even though it is not eternal; indeed both the beginning of Genesis and the first verses of John's Gospel explicitly state this (*cf.* Mk. 13:31). Mrs Eddy, however, writes: 'Spirit is the only substance and consciousness recognized by divine Science. The material senses oppose this, but there are no material senses, for matter has no mind' (p.278). If we ask what then matter is, her answer is, 'Matter is a human concept' (p.469). More about the Christian approach to these issues will be found at the end of this chapter. Note, incidentally, how Mormonism comes down on the opposite side, and holds that matter is so much a reality that even God must have a material body.

It is obvious that Mrs Eddy has parted company with the Bible, since the opening chapters of Genesis clearly show that God created this very material world. Moreover the incarnation was Christ's taking of a fully material body and becoming subject to the laws of matter, by suffering hunger, thirst, pain and death. The answer of *Science and Health with Key to the Scriptures* is to spiritualize all references to material creation. In other words, Mrs Eddy first forms her theory, and then bends the Bible to fit it. Thus on Genesis 1:6 she says, 'Spiritual understanding, by which human conception, material sense, is separated from Truth, is the firmament' (p.505). On Genesis 1:16, 'The sun is a metaphorical representation of Soul outside the body, giving existence and intelligence to the universe' (p.510). The very earthy Genesis 2 is brushed aside as 'false history in contradistinction to the true. . . . In this erroneous theory, matter takes the place of Spirit. Matter is represented as the life-giving principle of

74

the earth' (p.522). We find an extraordinary interpretation of Adam. 'Divide the name Adam into two syllables, and it reads, *a dam*, or obstruction. This suggests the thought of something fluid, of mortal mind in solution' (p.338). On similarly fanciful lines we could find a warning against Christian Science in Ephesians 4:14, where we are told not to be carried about with every wind of doctrine; and a wind of this kind is often called an *eddy*!

The book objects to the title Jehovah, which appears in Genesis 2 for the first time. 'Did the divine and infinite Principle become a finite deity, that He should now be called Jehovah?' (p.524). On the same page the worship of Jehovah is compared to the worship of pagan deities. Certainly the Old Testament prophets denounced the virtual equation of the two forms of worship in popular thought and practice, but they held firmly to the revelation of Jehovah as the personal God (*e.g.* the great vision in Isaiah 6). And Jesus Christ Himself quoted the Old Testament command that we should love Jehovah our God with all our being (Mk. 12:29,30).

Mortal mind

Matter is said to be 'a human concept' (p.469), the product of Mortal Mind which is under the delusion that disease, which appears as an affliction of the body, is real. The term, Mortal Mind, occurs frequently, but it is extremely difficult to say exactly what it means. 'It is meant to designate that which has no real existence' (p.114). Matter is said to be 'another name for mortal mind' (p.591). A definition says, 'MORTAL MIND. Nothing claiming to be something, for Mind is immortal . . . the opposite of Spirit, and therefore the opposite of God, or good; the belief that life has a beginning and therefore an end . . . the subjective states of error; material senses; that which neither exists in Science nor can be recognized by the spiritual sense; sin; sickness; death' (pp.591, 592). Once again one notes that everything turns on Mrs Eddy's own idea that Spirit cannot create genuinely existing matter.

Christian Science denies the reality of sin and sickness, and it is significant that these two are regularly linked by Mrs Eddy, as in the above quotation. Thus, 'The only reality of sin, sickness, or death is the awful fact that unrealities seem real to human, erring belief, until God strips off their disguises' (p.472). 'Christ came to destroy the belief of sin' (p.473). 'Jesus bore our infirmities; he knew the error of mortal belief, and "with his stripes (the rejection of error) we are healed"' (p.20). The above phrase 'he knew the error of mortal belief' is ambiguous, but its meaning is clear on page 53; 'At the time when Jesus felt our infirmities, he had not conquered all the beliefs of the flesh or his sense of material life.'

This astonishing interpretation of the redemptive work of Christ must be seen against the idea that man is not a fallen being. 'Whatever indicates the fall of man or the opposite of God or God's absence, is the Adam-man, for it is not begotten of the Father' (p.282). Moreover, 'Sin exists here or hereafter only as long as the illusion of mind in matter remains. It is a sense of sin, and not a sinful soul, which is lost' (p.311). In contradiction of this idea the Bible contains Christ's awful warning to 'fear him who can destroy both soul and body in hell' (Mt. 10:28); and sin is not an illusion, but a hideous stain from which we must be made clean (1 Jn.1:7).

Christian Science leaders today are naturally concerned to expound Mrs Eddy's teachings in a way that makes more sense. Thus a representative of the Committee on Publication wrote in a personal letter, 'The words "unreal" and "real" have a distinct meaning in Christian Science. The word "real" relates only to what is *divinely* true. When, therefore, the Christian Science textbook refers to sickness as "unreal", it certainly does not imply that it has no existence in human affairs. As much space is taken up to show how cancer, tuberculosis, brain disease, insanity *etc.* are to be treated in Christian Science, it is obvious that they are not being regarded as non-existent or unreal in a *human* sense. The thing which no doubt encouraged Mary Baker Eddy to class disease as "unreal" in the *divine* sense was the fact that it disappeared immediately it was confronted by the divine understanding of our Lord. So the word "unreal" in Christian Science has the definite Pauline sense that "the things which are seen are temporal" (2 Cor. 4:18).'

Similarly the writer points out that Christian Science makes people aware of their sins, which must be seen and cast out. But 'from a *divine* standpoint sin is as "unreal" to God as "three threes are ten" is unreal to mathematical principle. . . . The word "unreal" is applied to sin as to sickness to indicate "no part of spiritual reality" rather than "no existence as a factor in human affairs".'

We have quoted extensively from this letter, sent to one of the authors, so as to try to understand a possible difference between existence and reality. All one can say is that we do not find this difference in the Bible. Paul's words quoted from 2 Corinthians 4:18 do not deny the reality of the temporal, but rather affirm it, although it is impermanent, and will one day give place to the eternal, in which already we may have a part. Neither sin nor disease is anywhere cured in the Bible by denying its reality; both are realities in the mind of God and man, and both have to be overcome. Once again, it is theory first in Christian Science, and Scripture afterwards.

There is at least one practical refutation of these ideas about Mortal Mind and illness. If someone eat or drinks something poisonous, believing in his mortal mind that it is innocuous, he may continue to be unaware of the facts until the poison kills him. Mrs Eddy's ingenious explanation on pages 177, 178 is, 'In such cases a few persons believe the potion swallowed by the patient to be harmless, but the vast majority of mankind, though they know nothing of this particular case and this special person, believe the arsenic, the strychnine, or whatever the drug used, to be poisonous, for it is set down as a poison by mortal mind. Consequently, the result is controlled by the majority of opinions, not by the infinitesimal minority of opinions in the sick-chamber.' One wonders how far a Christian Scientist would stretch this to cover the case some years ago when several babies died through an unknown fault in the dried milk they were given.

It is very difficult to discover what Mrs Eddy believed about death. The laudatory biography, *The Cross and the Crown* by Norman Beasley, does not even record Mrs Eddy's death! Yet she and other good Christian Scientists have certainly died, although 'matter and death are mortal illusions' (p.289). It would seem from pages 44ff. that Jesus Himself did not actually die. His disciples believed that His body was dead, but in fact 'He met and mastered on the basis of Christian Science, the power of Mind over matter'. He refused to recognize death, and consequently His body remained alive until He emerged from the tomb (p.45).

So far as the rest of us are concerned, our bodies seem to die and 'the corpse, deserted by thought, is cold and decays, but it never suffers. . . . Mortals waken from the dream of death with bodies unseen by those who think that they bury the body' (p.429). This approximates in experience to what any Christian believes without tangling it up with Christian Science philosophy.

The remainder of this chapter must consider the ideas concerning God and Jesus Christ.

God

God is defined as 'Principle; Mind; Soul; Spirit; Life; Truth; Love; all substance; intelligence' (p.587). 'God, Spirit, is All-in-all, and there is no other might nor mind' (p.275).

This comes very close to Pantheism and to the Hindu concept of all separate existences as illusion. Pantheism is the concept that God is all and all is God. Mrs Eddy limits Pantheism to the belief 'that there is mind in matter' (p.279) and 'that God, or Life, is in or of matter' (p.27). Even though one dismisses matter as an illusion, one may still be pantheistic, if one holds that all existence is spirit, and that there is only one spirit, namely God.

Belief in the Trinity is summarized as follows: 'God the Father-Mother; Christ the spiritual idea of sonship; divine science or the Holy Comforter' (p.331). One need not dispute the mother aspects of God's being, since women as well as men were created in the image of God (Gn. 1:27), although the Bible nowhere addresses God as Mother. The interpretation of the Holy Spirit as divine Science (*i.e.* Christian Science) has scant regard for what the New Testament teaches of His personal being.

Jesus Christ
The Christian Science concept of Jesus Christ needs some disentangling, and one must continually watch the use of the two names, Jesus and Christ. Christian Science joins the ranks of those who do not believe in the incarnation as it is summed up in Scripture. Rather, there is first a human Jesus; then at some point something is added to him, known as the Christ, or Christ spirit. A heading on page 473 is 'Jesus not God', and on the same page we read, 'Jesus is the name of the man who, more than all other men, has presented Christ, the true idea of God.' While on earth 'the eternal Christ, his spiritual selfhood, never suffered' (p.38). There is a fuller treatment of these and similar concepts elsewhere in our chapter on 'Theosophical Systems'.

One can see now more clearly the reason for the inadequate treatment of the *atonement*, already referred to. We have also seen that the resurrection of Jesus Christ is not regarded as the rising again of His material, though transformed, body from its real death on the cross. But at the ascension 'the human, material concept, or Jesus, disappeared, while the spiritual self, or Christ, continues to exist in the eternal order of divine Science' (p.334). By contrast, the New Testament looks forward to the time when 'at the name of *Jesus* every knee shall bow . . . and every tongue confess that *Jesus Christ* is Lord . . . ' (Phil. 2:10,11).

To sum up: Christian Science is scientific in the sense that it uses well-established laws for healthy and health-giving thinking, and practises proved social and individual morality. As a religio-philosophical system it takes its place among alternative philosophies, and can fairly be compared with them. But as an exposition of biblical truth it is very far from the mark.

A Christian approach to points at issue

Spirit and matter
God is Spirit (Jn. 4:24), but He is also the Creator of this very real space-time universe, involving that which is material (Gn. 1 and 2; Acts 17:24, and frequently in Scripture). Since it requires tortuous thinking in the face of human experience to dismiss the material as unreal, it is hard to see why God should have put us all under this delusion. Note that the Bible regards spirit and matter as equally real. Sin and the world system have to be overcome, not by denying their reality, but by struggling against them (e.g. Jn. 16:33). The Christian Scientist must be asked to say why spirit could not create matter.

The nature of God
The Bible teaching concerning the Trinity (see Appendix) is completely different from that of Christian Science, as quoted in this chapter.

Healing
Undoubtedly God does heal beyond what medical science would expect, but it is not His will to heal everyone (e.g. 2 Tim. 4:20). The Christian recognizes that God has implanted in all of us a movement towards life and wholeness, and, when we are ill, we look for healing. We use such God-given methods as will best assist the healing powers of the body. The doctor will diagnose and prescribe for what is really wrong. Or positive thinking may assist the body to rally. We pray to God to use either or both of these factors, or at times to work without the use of means. There is no single case in Scripture of any cure through denying the real existence of the illness. A Christian has no reason to deny the effects of thought on the body, and to a certain extent Mrs Eddy accepted this, although she considered only the effects

of wrong thinking. Her system would not allow her to treat her healings as the results of mind over matter. Hence she opposed any suggestion of what she called 'animal magnetism', which is something rather wider than hypnotism, although she admitted that it could produce results, as we have seen in this chapter. See especially page 484 of *Science and Health*.

To try to summarize forms of healing: Attempts to heal disease may be by three means.

1. By treating it as materially real to be overcome by material means, *e.g.* through doctors and surgeons. Matter is thus considered as real as spirit.

2. By the influence of mind on matter, *e.g.* through faith-healing which also treats illness as a real state from which one needs deliverance.

3. By Christian Science in which 'the physical affirmation of disease should always be met by the mental negation' (p.392).

One should note, finally, that Christian Scientists, or, as they often prefer to call themselves, Students of Christian Science, are good and gracious people who have no desire to engage in belligerent controversy. Orthodox Christians might sometimes take a leaf from their book.

Note

About books

There is no substitute for Mrs Eddy's own writings, published by the Christian Science Publishing Society, including *Science and Health with Key to the Scriptures*, *Miscellaneous Writings* (1883–1896) and *The First Church of Christ, Scientist, and Miscellany* (published in 1913 by her trustees after her death). Both of these last two books contain much informative material, philosophical, historical and anecdotal, and the last named also contains some original poems.

It is probably impossible to find a 'neutral' biography of Mrs Eddy. Laudatory books include: Norman Beasley, *The Cross and the Crown* (Hawthorn Books, 1952); *Mary Baker*

Eddy (1964); *The Continuing Spirit – since* 1910 (Allen and Unwin, 1957); Robert Peel, *Mary Baker Eddy: the Years of Discovery to 1870* (Holt, Rinehart and Winston, 1966); Sibyl Wilbur, *The Life of Mary Baker Eddy* (Concord, 1909); and C. S. Braden, *Christian Science Today* (Allen and Unwin, 1959).

On the other side, highly critical books include: Georgine Milmine, *Life of Mary Baker Eddy* (Doubleday, 1909); Edward F. Dakin, *Mrs Eddy* (Scribner's, 1930); W. R. Martin and N. H. Klann, *The Christian Science Myth* (Zondervan, 1955). An interesting work in this category is Mark Twain, *Christian Science and the Book of Mrs Eddy*, a typical Mark Twain extravaganza, printed among his collected articles and followed by a book in 1907. Stephen Leacock's Life of Mark Twain speaks of his 'queer obsession with Christian Science', which he thought 'was about to envelop the world'.

6 Spiritualism

SPIRITUALISM is not spiritual in the New Testament sense (*e.g.* 1 Cor. 2:10–16), but since this is the title that its advocates have chosen, we shall use it in this book. The derogatory term, *Spiritism*, is equally misleading, since it would imply that all the manifestations come from the spirit world, and this is not so.

What is Spiritualism?
Spiritualism claims to provide communication with the spirits of the departed. Usually the communication comes through a medium. He or she often goes into a trance, and consequently remembers nothing of what happened while the spirits took over their voice. It is usual for each medium to have one or more 'control spirits', often with strange names, who interpret or introduce other spirits who wish to contact someone at the seance. At other times the medium remains conscious but becomes aware of forms and voices that seem to be those of the departed who wish to communicate. Sometimes at private seances there are physical manifestations, such as objects being moved. Again at some such seances forms and faces appear to build up from a semi-physical substance known as ectoplasm, which is exuded or extruded from the body of the medium. The almost total darkness in which these seances are held has lent itself again and again to deception. Nowadays it is possible to see in the dark by means of an infra-red telescope or viewer, and

to take photographs with infra-red film. For this the room is lit with lamps which emit infra-red rays only, which to normal sight leaves the surroundings in darkness. Under these conditions physical mediums are reluctant to offer themselves for test, even with the prospect of considerable financial reward.

There is also a kind of 'do-it-yourself' mediumship using table-tipping, the ouija board, the planchette, or inverted tumbler. When hands or fingers are rested on these things and questions asked, a 'spirit' answers by causing the board to move to letters of the alphabet, or by rapping or thumping the table according to a prearranged code.

Interest in modern spiritualism in America and Europe dates from the middle of the last century when two sisters, Maggie and Kate Fox, appeared to be the centre of mysterious rappings. They and their elder sister, Leah, set up as mediums. Later in life Maggie and Kate confessed that they had faked the phenomena, but afterwards withdrew their confession. Their minds at that time were affected by heavy drinking, and it is impossible now to know the truth.

Biblical assessment

Spiritualism itself goes back to the distant past. It has always flourished among animistic peoples, but it was also well known in the Near East in Bible times. A Christian assessment starts with the knowledge that it is always forbidden in Scripture. The AV did not make this clear in its reference to 'familiar spirits', which at the time were believed to be animal-like demons who acted as the servants of witches. The RSV correctly uses the term 'mediums'. Rather strangely, the NEB and the Jerusalem Bible speak of 'consulting ghosts', which once again makes the warning sound irrelevant, since no-one consults ghosts as such. One cannot help but think that some translators deliberately try to play down the attack on mediumship.

There are several passages in the Law that are most emphatic. Thus Deuteronomy 18:10,11 gives a full list of banned practices. 'There shall not be found among you . . .

any one who practises divination, a soothsayer, or an augur, or a sorcerer, or a charmer, or a medium, or a wizard, or a necromancer.' Some of these have nothing to do with spirits, but divine from signs, or work spells. But the last three involve those who claimed to make contact with the spirits of the departed.

It was the duty of the king to put away mediums. Saul removed them in 1 Samuel 28:3, and so did Josiah in 2 Kings 23:24. The evil king Manasseh supported them (2 Ki. 21:6). There is a strong condemnation in the prophetic books, when Isaiah 8:19,20 declares, 'When they say to you, "Consult the mediums and the wizards who chirp and mutter," (a reference to the changed voices of the man or woman in trance) should not a people consult their God? Should they consult the dead on behalf of the living? To the teaching and to the testimony! Surely for this word which they speak there is no dawn.'

The Hebrew word translated 'medium' is *ob*, which in fact has primary reference to the control spirit itself. This is demonstrated in 1 Samuel 28:7, where the medium of Endor is described literally as an 'owner of an *ob*'. But for clarity the translation 'medium' is justified, just as a person today might speak of consulting the spirits when he means to consult a medium.

There are two ways suggested of evading the Old Testament ban.

1. It is claimed that the mediums referred to were impostors. It is true that the Jews who translated the Hebrew scriptures into Greek (*i.e.* the Septuagint, or LXX) used the Greek word corresponding to 'ventriloquist' for these mediums. But that does not mean a modern stage ventriloquist, an obvious pretender, as is sometimes argued. A study of the usages of the Greek word outside the LXX shows that it is always used of those who were believed to be possessed by a spirit, *i.e.* a medium. They were not frauds.

2. It is argued that we are to be guided by the New Testament rather than by the Old, and that the New Testament does not forbid mediumship. A more important

fact however is that it nowhere advocates it. This is more than an argument from silence, for the New Testament always assumes the authority of the Old Testament and its teaching as given by God. While it makes clear when Old Testament law is fulfilled or abrogated (as was the ritual and sacrificial law by Christ's coming), its silence over the law concerning mediums implies agreement with it. Moreover, in two places Paul comforts those who have lost loved ones (1 Thes. 4:13–18; 1 Cor. 15:12–20). Now spiritualists believe that New Testament prophets were Christian mediums. If this were so, Paul need only have invited the bereaved to come and contact the departed at a Christian meeting. In fact, he comforts them with the assurance that both they and their loved ones are in Christ, and Christ is risen from the dead.

The medium of Endor in 1 Samuel 28 is capable of two explanations. One is that she faked the seance, but this is hardly the impression that one receives from the way in which 'Samuel' speaks. The other, and more probable, is that God allowed Samuel to return, even under these conditions, and the medium was taken aback at the different type of spirit from that which she normally experienced (verse 12).

There is no reason why for some purpose God should not allow a departed person to return in a visible form, as He did with Samuel, and again with Moses and Elijah on the mount of transfiguration. Jesus Christ Himself accepted the fact that spirits might appear (Lk. 24:37–39), but said that their form was not the same as His own, since He was in His body, risen and transformed; they were still awaiting their resurrection. In the story of Dives and Lazarus (Lk. 16: 19–31) it is not said that Lazarus could not have been sent back to warn the rich man's brothers, but that it was not right for him to return to those who already had the clear guidance of the Scriptures.

Spontaneous appearances, then, are one thing, but attempts to make further contact come under the Bible ban. One can see three possible reasons for the ban.

1. Contact with spirits easily becomes a substitute for vital Christian experience. Spiritualists make much of a report drawn up by Archbishop Lang's Committee in 1938. This was never published, but *Psychic News* somehow obtained a copy of the conclusions, though not of the evidence, and published it as a booklet. In fact the report satisfies neither spiritualists nor evangelical Christians. But it includes these words: 'We were impressed by the unsatisfactory answers received from practising Spiritualists to such questions as "Has your prayer life, your sense of God, been strengthened by your spiritualistic experiences?" . . . Spiritualism may afford men the opportunity of escaping the challenge of faith which, when truly proclaimed, makes so absolute a claim upon men's lives that they will not face it, but turn aside to an easier way.'

2. Many of the apparent messages from the departed may well be drawn from the memories of the bereaved by a medium's second sight. Most people who have seriously examined the evidence for extra-sensory perception (ESP) are convinced that it can occur. One of the best known mediums of recent times, the late Mrs Eileen Garrett, several times expressed her belief that the many thousands of communications that came through her were drawn from the subconscious minds of her clients. This does not mean that she faked them, any more than the clairvoyant fakes the pictures that seem to appear in the crystal, but the stored memories and feelings come to her from the bereaved as pictures and voices. In her book *Many Voices* published not long before her death, she takes a completely agnostic position with regard to survival after death. If she is right – and at least she holds this opinion after a lifetime of introspective investigation – the comfort that comes to the bereaved is a credit to their own love and affection rather than a direct communication from the departed. It neither proves nor disproves their survival, but it is in fact deceptive.

3. Those who plunge more deeply into spiritualist investigations find that the communications gradually draw them away from the essentials of the Christian faith. In the

87

last century the Rev. Stainton Moses wrote one or two books of spirit teachings that show how he was gradually led to deny these fundamentals. This is well recognized by all serious investigators. Thus Lord Dowding in *Many Mansions* points out that 'the doctrine of the Trinity seems to have no adherents in advanced circles of the spirit world'. Jesus Christ is a Son of God just as we are sons of God. The doctrine of remission of sins through the atoning death of Christ is, he says, vigorously denied.

The rejection of these supreme revealed truths brings Christianity to the level of other world religions. Yet they formed the distinctive good news of the gospel which spread like wildfire after Pentecost. It almost looks as though some enemy is anxious to cut them out in defiance of God. In fact the New Testament shows that there are these enemies, Satan and other rebel spirits. Satan struggled to keep Jesus Christ from going to the cross, since His sacrificial death there was the only means of bringing man from death to life, and from darkness to light, and thus breaking Satan's hold upon him (*e.g.* Jn. 12:31,32). Thus in the wilderness and through Simon Peter Satan offered Christ alternatives to Calvary (Lk. 4:6,7; Mt. 16:22,23). After Christ's triumph Satan and his agents continue the battle by deception (2 Cor. 4:4; Rev. 12:9 *etc.*) and persecution (1 Pet. 5:8–10).

Their deception includes false messages from above (1 Jn. 4:1–6; 1 Tim. 4:1). Spiritualists warn against the danger of deception by evil spirits, but claim that they test the spirits as 1 John 4:1–6 orders. We discuss the exact nature of this test in the chapter on *Theosophical Systems*, but the relevant point here is that the test is not to establish whether the spirit is your good grandfather or some evil spirit impersonating him, but whether the spirit in the prophet is the Holy Spirit of God or some evil spirit trying to put over some teaching that reduces Christ to purely human level.

Allied phenomena

Recently there has been a revival of interest in the ouija board. Clearly some force moves the board to spell out answers to questions when two or three rest their fingers on it. The makers do not claim more than a force that comes from one's own subconscious mind. In practice the questions are asked of some entity outside of oneself, and the answers claim to be given by some departed spirit, who often identifies himself as someone who was known to a member of the group in his lifetime. Those who move in student and teenage circles have met enough damage to personality via the ouija board or sliding tumbler to make them extremely suspicious of the real source of the messages. Some young people have been encouraged to attempt suicide. Others have had most frightening inner experiences and compulsions. At times a haunting sense of evil has hung about the environment after seances have been held. Where Christians have been aware of this sort of seance and have prayed definitely against it in the name of Jesus Christ, the movements of the board have ceased, whereas a good spirit would have been assisted by Christian prayers. Since the board does not move by itself, the spirit must enter into you in order to draw on your inner forces, and once the door has been deliberately opened, it cannot easily be closed again. In fact only the claiming of the victory of Jesus Christ can give full deliverance.

In the next few years more will certainly be heard of alleged spirit communications through tape recorders connected to radio. The publicizing has come through a Latvian, Dr Raudive, but much experimental work has been done in Britain, and particularly in Dublin. There is no doubt that voices are found to be imprinted on a tape when it has been run back, and the apparatus of top electronic experts has eliminated any chance of fraud or error. In response to a thought or a spoken request, the 'spirit' is found to have spoken a few words, which then must be amplified and interpreted against the heavy background noise (*cf*. Konstantin Raudive, *Breakthrough*; Peter Bander, *Keep on Talking*).

It would be foolish to venture on a firm explanation at this stage, but there are one or two relevant considerations.

First, the voices are of only a few words, and, having heard them on a record, one can find a distinct resemblance to the snatches of words that one sometimes hears mentally when in a half-doze. Secondly, there is a resemblance to the un-explained feat of Ted Serios in America, who under the strictest control by experts has been able by mental con-centration to produce photographs of other parts of the world on polaroid film. He is not a medium (*cf.* J. Eisenbud, *The World of Ted Serios*). May it not be that the Raudive voices belong to a similar unexplained category? It is no harder to conceive that the mind of a living person can imprint a sentence or picture than that a spirit can do so. Thus, having desired to contact a friend in the next world, one mentally formulates his voice and characteristic words, and this appears on the tape when it is played back, although it cannot be heard while the tape is being monitored as it is run through.

Life after death

If it is said that spiritualism is an ally of Christianity since it has proved survival after death, mere survival is not what interests the Christian. Survival is not the same as the eternal life of the New Testament. It is no more than a rewriting of the well-known saying from Isaiah 22:13, 'Let us eat and drink, for tomorrow we do not die.' The good news of Jesus Christ was not that everyone survived death, but that the new quality life of God, eternal life, was to be found in Him here and now. That is why the Christian rests on the his-torical fact of Christ's resurrection as his guarantee, and not upon communications from the departed. It is true that the New Testament reveals almost nothing about the present life of the departed until they receive their new bodies at the second coming of Christ, but it does reveal that they are 'with Christ' in a state which is 'far better' than the highest bliss of earthly existence (Phil. 1:23).

Notes

About books

It is impossible to try to list the many thousands of books on spiritualism and, in recent times, the related subject of ESP.

Good surveys of the field are: G. N. M. Tyrrell, *The Personality of Man* (Pelican, 1945); W. H. Salter, *Zoar* (Sidgwick and Jackson, 1961) which is a careful summary of how much and how little has been proved by spiritualism; D. J. West, *Psychical Research Today* (Pelican. 1962), a down-to-earth critique; Charles McCreery, *Science, Philosophy, and ESP* (Faber, 1967); and most recently Arthur Koestler, *The Roots of Coincidence* (Hutchinson, 1972), a discussion in the light of modern physics.

Two evangelical assessments are: J. Stafford Wright, *Mind, Man, and the Spirits* (Paternoster, 1972) which was originally entitled *What is Man?*, and, by the same author, *Christianity and the Occult* (Scripture Union, 1971).

One of the most thought-provoking writers from the Christian standpoint is Professor H. H. Price, who, as philosopher, discusses the concept of survival, and also the relation between ESP and religious experience including prayer. His *Essays in the Philosophy of Religion* (Oxford University Press, 1972) is most stimulating.

7 Theosophical Systems

FOR MOST people Theosophy means the Theosophical
Society. But, if one spells the word without the capital,
theosophy characterizes a series of religious and semi-
religious systems. What binds these together is their claim to
hold a tradition that has been handed down among initiates
for thousands of years. They have a high regard for Jesus
Christ, and hold that He knew these same truths. Some say
that He was initiated into them in Egypt. Since He taught
them secretly to His disciples, they are not found in the
Gospels. In the early church too they were taught to an
inner circle only, but they were also known to the Gnostics.

The main systems

At the present time the main expressions of theosophy are
found in the Theosophical Society, Anthroposophy, Rosicrucianism, Advanced Occultism, sometimes the Higher
Spiritualism, and also in the teachings of Edgar Cayce.
We may look at these in turn before discussing specific
teachings.

The Theosophical Society

This was founded in New York in 1875 by Colonel H. S.
Olcott (1832–1907) and Madame H. P. Blavatsky (1831–
1891). They claimed guidance from reincarnated teachers
in the Himalayas. Mrs Annie Besant (1847-1933) succeeded
them, and was assisted for a time by C. W. Leadbeater, who

later became bishop of the so-called Liberal Catholic Church. All three main leaders spent some time in India, and were influenced by Hinduism and Buddhism.

The stated aims of the Society are:

1. To form a nucleus of Universal Brotherhood of Humanity, without distinction of race, creed, sex, caste, or colour.

2. To encourage the study of comparative religion, philosophy, and science.

3. To investigate the unexplained laws of nature and the powers latent in man.

Anthroposophy

In 1912 Mrs Besant announced that a Hindu boy, Krishnamurti, was the reincarnation of the Supreme World Teacher. This claim, later repudiated by Krishnamurti himself, led to the withdrawal of Rudolf Steiner (1861-1925) from the Society, who thereafter developed what he named Anthroposophy, which owed more to the west than the east. Although Anthroposophy means 'human wisdom' in contradistinction to Theosophy, or 'God wisdom', Steiner is closer to the Christian faith than Mrs Besant. He had remarkable intuitive awareness, and has impressed many serious people as a great man, rather than a crank.

Rudolf Steiner schools, including those for the mentally retarded, employ unusual but effective methods, based on what Steiner believed about the inner development of the child. The effectiveness of the schools neither proves nor disproves the esoteric beliefs of Steiner himself.

Rosicrucianism

Between 1614 and 1616 four booklets were published describing the travels of a certain man named Christian Rosenkreuz (Rosycross), and his initiation into occult secrets. Originally he may have been intended as an allegorical rather than a historical character. A Lutheran pastor, J. V. Andreae, probably wrote at least one of the booklets. In the eighteenth century Rosicrucian Societies were formed in Europe, and became closely associated with Freemasonry.

Today Masonic Lodges have an optional degree, the Rose Croix of Heredom.

In 1865 Wentworth Little founded the Societas Rosicruciana in Anglia, with eight degrees limited to Freemasons. Soon after 1900 H. Spencer Lewis founded the Ancient Mystical Order Rosae Crucis (AMORC). With its headquarters in California, this is the group that continually advertises its postal courses in reputable periodicals. It has a rival in the less secretive group founded by Max Heindel early in the present century.

Advanced Occultism

We use this term to distinguish its followers from practising magicians. It is not a society or group, but represents a religio-philosophic exploration of man and the universe, generally by 'freelances', with a basis of theosophical ideas.

Higher Spiritualism

We use this term to distinguish it from the run-of-the-mill spiritualism of the local circles and churches where people hope to receive messages from some departed loved one. Some researchers have little time for this, but try to contact spirits who will speak of experiences, conditions and ideas that throw light on the whole course of man's journey in time. Such alleged communicators range from Malachi to F. W. H. Myers, and their messages are basically theosophical, though there are differences between them, notably over reincarnation.

Edgar Cayce (1876–1944)

Cayce was a devout American evangelical, who under trance was able to diagnose and prescribe for illnesses in a remarkable way. He made no claims to mediumship or spirit guidance. In 1923 his gift was exploited by a certain Arthur Lammers whose mind was crammed with theosophical ideas, which Cayce in trance confirmed. From this time onwards Cayce expounded similar ideas, including some that are very strange indeed. One may suggest that, just as Cayce in trance found an inner identification with the deep mind of sick patients, so now he unconsciously identified with the inner mind of Lammers. Since Cayce's death his trance dictations and deductions from them have been published in books and periodicals by the Association for Research and Enlightenment of Virginia Beach, USA.

Main ideas

The following are some of the main theosophical ideas:

Reincarnation

The systems differ over the number and frequency of rebirths, and also over their purpose. The Theosophical Society follows the east in emphasizing the law in *karma*, according to which all our experiences in this life are in precise accord with the reward and punishment that we have deserved in all our previous lives.

What we make of our present life will be carried on to subsequent lives in a similar way. The other systems stress the multiplicity of experiences that we can gain on the way to maturity. When we enter a fresh life, we choose, or are allotted, a family situation in which we can best develop along hitherto unexperienced lines, or relearn lessons that we have failed to learn before.

One naturally asks about Jesus. Only Steiner believes that He had no more than one incarnation. Cayce under trance discovered some thirty incarnations for Him, including one as Adam. The Theosophical Society and Occultists believe in Masters, or Adepts, including Jesus, who have completed all the incarnations that they need, but who may choose to remain on earth to be guides and helpers. According to Cyril Scott in *An Outline of Modern Occultism*, Jesus is now alive in a Syrian body in Lebanon.

It is generally thought that the incarnations began in the far distant past, and that the lost continents of Lemuria and Atlantis were important centres of civilized development. Man's evolution has been guided by great spiritual beings, who had themselves evolved into an equivalent of cells in the Divine Being who is at work in our solar system. This is worked out by Steiner, the Rosicrucians, and Cayce. There is no common agreement over the number and frequency of the incarnations, even among those who claim to have a direct perception of the previous lives of themselves and others.

In recent years attempts have been made by hypnotists to take people back into memories of previous lives. Some subjects in this highly suggestible state will easily romanticize. Others produce buried memories of what they have been read or been told. Thus the apparent memories of an American housewife of her life in Ireland in the last century as Bridey Murphy shook America in 1956, until it transpired that they were almost certainly romanticized derivations of stories she had heard from her Irish aunt when she was a little girl.

Where there is no evidence at all of buried memories there is yet another possibility, which one may draw from the theosophical systems themselves. This is that every event in history is imprinted on past time and can be picked up by certain people under certain conditions. One can see a special example of this in hauntings, where long-dead characters are seen or heard re-enacting parts that once they played. It is unlikely that the murderer and his victim are brought back in person on each occasion! Cayce claimed that in trance he was taken to a symbolic library, where all the volumes of an individual's life records were stored. By extracting the volume, he became aware of all the lives that the person had passed through. We may, however, suggest that in fact Cayce was able to slip into past time, and pick up the experiences of some individual, whom he then erroneously supposed to be the client who was consulting him.

Although most apparent memories go back to previous lives that were lived many years ago, there are cases in India especially where a child 'remembers' having recently been one of a family – perhaps father or grandfather – in some village in another part of the country. He describes and names his former relatives, and he is proved to be correct when he is taken to the village he names. Telepathy with his new parents is ruled out, since they have no knowledge of the other family. Yet there may be a freak telepathic link of the child with the other family, corresponding to a link of feeling which certain clairvoyants have when they speak of someone whom they do not know, but about whom they have been consulted. Some support for this theory may be found in one case where the person who seemed to be reincarnated did not die until some three and a half years after the child with the memories was born. About twenty cases were examined by Dr Ian Stevenson, and published by the American Society for Psychical Research in 1966.

Why should a Christian object to reincarnation? There is the plain text that it is appointed for men to die once only (Heb. 9:27,28). But, more significantly, if the belief is true it must affect our whole understanding of life and salvation. Yet Jesus Christ nowhere introduced it into His teaching. Theosophists say that He did teach it secretly, and His disciples passed it on in secret. By such reasoning one can make out that Christ taught anything one chooses! The references to John the Baptist as Elijah are explained by Luke 1:17 where John is described as preparing the way 'in the spirit and power of Elijah'.

Jesus Christ

Most of these systems distinguish Jesus from the Christ, as also does Christian Science. The Christ may be the Logos, or Mind of God at work in mankind, so that one can speak of the Christ in every man. Rosicrucians regard the Christ as the supreme initiate of a certain period in the development of the universe. Rosicrucians and Steiner accept a belief that was early rejected by Christian theologians, namely that the Christ descended in fullness on the man Jesus at His baptism. Thus there was no proper incarnation, but something equivalent to the filling of the prophets by the Spirit of God.

It is important to note the test in 1 John 4:2,3 for true or false revelations that profess to come from God. 'By this you know the Spirit of God: every spirit which confesses that Jesus Christ has come in the flesh is of God, and every spirit which does not confess Jesus is not of God' – *i.e.* an incarnation, and not a separation of Jesus from the Christ. There is actually an early variation in the Greek text, and although it is unlikely to be the original, it emphasizes the meaning of the true text and it was quoted by several early Christian writers, and in its Latin form appears in the Vulgate. This variation has, 'Every spirit which looses (or divides) Jesus is not of God.' We may interpret 1 John 5:6 in a similar way. 'This is he who came by water and blood, Jesus Christ (note both names), not with the water only but with the water and the blood.' At first sight one thinks of the blood of atonement, but in John 1:13 blood stands for conception and birth. Thus Jesus was not only designated as Messiah at His baptism when He was called to commence His public ministry, but was also the one Jesus Christ from conception. (See also the Appendix on the Trinity.)

Atonement

The Theosophical Society, following Hindu and Buddhist ideas, adopts a doctrine of *karma* (exact and inevitable retribution or reward) which makes forgiveness and remission of sins impossible. In every lifetime we reap the reward or pay off the debts of previous lives. Many spiritualists agree. Cayce and Steiner accept *karma* up to a point, but believe that the death of Jesus Christ on the cross is central, and opens the way for forgiveness and redemption, so that bad *karma* may be broken.

Psychic powers

All these systems hold that man has latent powers which can be developed. The brochures of the Rosicrucian AMORC offer to teach their use. They include simple capacities like hunches and intuitions, telepathy and clairvoyance, thought projection, the reading of the past and the future, and such things as astral projection.

The careful investigations of psychical research have

shown that these capacities occasionally emerge spontaneously. The danger of trying to develop them is that at the least they become over-absorbing since they give a sense of power, and at the worst they become involved in mediumship. They may even be used in witchcraft, where the covens, or gatherings, of witches generate psychic power in order to project it for their own purposes.

Spirit beings

These systems have an active belief in unseen elementals and grades of spirits, good and bad. Sometimes these spirits merely form a background of belief, as with the *devas*, who are regarded as spirits who look after the world of nature. The Findhorn Trust in Scotland claims to have personal fellowship with these spirits in their efforts to grow good food and flowers.

On the other hand there are magicians and witches who try to make use of these spirits. The novels of Denis Wheatley show something of how they work, although Wheatley himself has never taken part in magical ceremonies. There are groups who practise what is called Ritual Magic, such as the Golden Dawn, and other magicians who operate as individuals. Generally there is a blend of psychic force and the invocation of spirits, but always there is the aim of God-like power.

It is likely that Colossians 2 speaks of magic of this kind. Paul takes the magician at his face value as one who is aiming at what is good. Hence the magician invokes angels (18) and undergoes the discipline that magicians inflict on themselves before approaching the unseen world (21). Paul attacks any practice that tries to make use of spirit beings, good or bad. His argument here is that Christ has delivered us from the elemental spirits of the universe (8, 20), those fallen spirits that try to sway the minds of men (2 Cor. 4:4 of the supreme rebel, Satan; and Eph. 6:12 of the world rulers of darkness). Further, in Colossians 2:15 Paul speaks of the disarming of the principalities and powers by Christ on the cross. Therefore he concludes that we are not to tamper with intermediate beings, whether professedly good or bad, since we are linked to Christ, the Head (9,10). If we are joined to the Head, what place is there for the in-betweens? The unadmitted answer is that submission to Christ means the desire to do His will; the manipulation of psychic and spirit forces means the power to do my own will.

Notes

About books
A fuller evangelical assessment of some of the occult forces mentioned here will be found in: J. Stafford Wright, *Mind, Man, and the Spirits* (formerly *What is Man?*) (Paternoster, 1972), and *Christianity and the Occult* (Scripture Union, 1971).

The seven-volume magazine, *Man, Myth and Magic* (Purnell, for the British Publishing Corporation, 1970–71) contains authoritative articles on the subjects mentioned in this chapter.

Books include the following:

The Theosophical Society publishes its own booklets. A critical treatment of its early days can be found in John Symonds, *Madame Blavatsky: Medium and Magician* (Odhams, 1959).

Anthroposophy. The Anthroposophical Society publishes Steiner's works. A good over-all idea of his teachings will be found in a volume of essays, A. C. Harwood (ed.), *The Faithful Thinker* (Hodder and Stoughton, 1961).

Rosicrucians. H. Spencer Lewis, *Rosicrucian Questions and Answers* (Rosicrucian Library, California, 1932).

Advanced Occultism. Cyril Scott, *Outline of Modern Occultism* (Routledge, 1949).

Ritual Magic. Francis King, *Ritual Magic in England* (Spearman, 1970).

Higher Spiritualism. Raynor Johnson, *Nurslings of Immortality* (Hodder and Stoughton, 1953) and *The Imprisoned Splendour* (Hodder and Stoughton, 1957).

Edgar Cayce. The standard life of Cayce is Thomas Sugrue, *There is a River* (Holt, Rinehart and Winston, 1942), now also in paperback (Dell, 1970). There are at least eight paperbacks of Cayce material, published in the USA, but often available in Britain.

8 Seventh-Day Adventism

THIS MOVEMENT had its origin in the middle of the last century, when there was an obsessive concern to explore the Bible, especially the book of Daniel, in order to discover the date of the second coming. Older readers will remember several similar attempts in the 1925–35 period, and Jehovah's Witnesses have foundered on this rock several times.

A prominent expositor in America was William Miller, who worked out that the second coming would be between March 1843 and March 1844. When his calculations proved useless, he fixed 22 October 1844, before becoming disillusioned.

Pastor Russell (see *Jehovah's Witnesses*) was also attracted by these calculations, as was a Mrs Ellen White, who claimed the gift of prophecy. Her solution was that Christ did indeed return in 1844, but not to earth. He went into the heavenly sanctuary to begin His investigative judgment. (See notes below.) Moreover she saw in her visions that the church was under God's displeasure for observing the first day of the week instead of the sabbath. Mrs White's prophecies were published in a number of books.

It is difficult to know how far modern Adventists accept all that Ellen White wrote. Their book, *Questions on Doctrine*, says that her writings are not in the same category as the Bible, but correspond to prophecies by men and women of Bible times which were not included in Scripture. The

Adventist writers do not deny any of her statements, but are at pains to remove what they believe are misinterpretations by orthodox Christians.

They originally obtained their name because of their belief in the imminence of the second coming. They retain it presumably because it would be difficult to change, but they also regard it as testifying to the Christian confidence in Christ's return.

Beliefs

Seventh-Day Adventism differs from the other faiths in this book in that it accepts the full Christian belief in the Trinity, the deity and incarnation of our Lord Jesus Christ, His atoning death on the cross, His bodily resurrection and ascension. A few of their biblical interpretations are unusual and need brief consideration, but their insistence on the observance of the Jewish sabbath rather than the first day of the week has been divisive in the Christian church, especially overseas, when their missionaries have gone into an area where there are already small communities who have been taught to observe the Lord's Day. There are a few other movements, such as the Armstrong 'World of Tomorrow', which also teach the observance of the Saturday sabbath.

The Sabbath

The standard Christian belief is that during New Testament times Christians came to observe the first day of the week, in memory of Christ's resurrection, and gradually ceased to observe the Saturday sabbath. Indications are as follows. 1. Acts 20:7. On the first day of the week the disciples gathered to break bread. 2. 1 Corinthians 16:2. Christians are told to lay aside whatever is right for the collection on the first day of the week. 3. Revelation 1:10. John is in the Spirit on the Lord's day. The Greek does not say 'the day of the Lord', but uses an adjective with the general meaning of 'belonging to the Lord'. Its only other occurrence in Scripture is in 1 Corinthians 11:20, 'the Lord's supper'. It is used of the first day of the week soon after New Testament times. Thus Ignatius in his Letter to the Magnesians 9:1 speaks of Christians as 'no longer observing sabbaths, but fashioning their lives after the Lord's day on which our life also rose through him'. The so-called Epistle of Barnabas, early in post-apostolic times, speaks of keeping 'the eighth day with joyfulness, the day on which Jesus rose from the dead' (15:9). Justin Martyr in the middle of the second century mentions the gathering of Christians on Sunday (Apology 1:67). There are several similar references which show that the first day was the regular day of Christian observance long before any Council decreed it. These are the indications on which the orthodox Christian rests. The first day was certainly observed soon after the New Testament was written; therefore we look for anything in the New Testament that would show that it was observed before the canon of Scripture was closed, and, as we have seen, the verses are there.

With this in mind we look at the Adventist case. We may dismiss as irrelevant the fact that Jesus Christ kept the sabbath, since this was before His resurrection. Similarly the visits of Paul and others to the synagogues on the sabbath were not for Christian worship, but to take advantage of the services in order to preach the gospel to the Jews. We are left with the strong argument that the sabbath is incorporated in the Ten Commandments, and, if we observe the rest of the commandments, we have no right to change this one. However, the New Testament does not agree. It quotes other commands from the Decalogue (Mk. 10:19; Rom. 13:8–10), but never the one on the sabbath. It goes further, and in Colossians 2:16,17 Paul says that no-one is to judge the Christian on matters of food and drink, or with regard to a festival or a new moon or a sabbath. This can only mean that the sabbath is no longer a normal part of the Christian calendar. Although Galatians 4:10 mentions 'days, and months, and seasons, and years' in general terms, it is likely that Paul included the Saturday sabbath here also.

The Adventist answer is that the reference in Colossians 2 is to the seven extra rest days that formed part of the festivals (*e.g.* Lv. 23:32). One would reply that it is absolutely impossible for a Hebrew like Paul to speak of sabbaths if he meant only seven days in the year and excluded the weekly sabbath. This would be even more so if he is writing to Gentiles, who certainly would know what the weekly sabbath was, but who would have little idea of the technical extra sabbaths of the law. We note also that Colossians 2:16, 17 links together the new moon and the sabbath, as is often done in the Old Testament, where there is no doubt that the weekly sabbath is referred to, the new moon being the regular first day of the month festival (*e.g.* Is. 1:13). Paul declares that the sabbath is a shadow, which is fulfilled in Christ (Col. 2:17). Two reasons are given in the law for observing the sabbath. In Exodus 20:11 it is in memory of God's completion of creation. In Deuteronomy 5:15 it is in memory of redemption from Egypt. These were shadows of the new creation and the full redemption that have come through Christ's death on the cross and its culmination in His resurrection on the first day.

It is right to point out that nowadays the Adventists do not say that sabbath keeping is necessary for salvation, nor that worshippers on Sunday have the mark of the beast upon them. They observe the sabbath out of loyalty to the expressed will of God. Needless to say, in rejecting the seventh day as the proper day for Christians to observe, we do not reject the principle of setting apart the first day as the Lord's day for worship, service, and rest. Experience has proved the value of God's creation ordinance in this respect.

Other Adventist ideas
Sabbath keeping is naturally the most important distinction of Adventism, but those who wish to explore some strange bypaths of interpretation will find the following:

1. Adventists hold a strange view of *Christ's investigative work in the heavenly sanctuary*. This, as we have seen, arose as a way out when Christ did not return in 1844. The simpler

way would have been to admit the failure of the calculations, as Miller himself did. Mrs White now saw that Christ had gone into the heavenly sanctuary to purify it. Daniel 8:14 was one of the precarious texts to support this view. The theory was that on the Day of Atonement the sin-stained blood was taken into the Holy of Holies (Lv. 16:14) and, according to the Adventists, the sin still needed to be removed from the blood. This was thought to be the type picture of what Christ is now doing, since 1844. In the heavenly sanctuary there are the actual records of every human life, and Christ is now destroying the records of the sins of the saved, which have already been forgiven. We may reply that typology does not allow us to build up a doctrine that is not clearly stated elsewhere. In Hebrews 9:24 the reference is to heaven, in contrast to an earthly sanctuary, and Christ returned there long before 1844.

2. *The scapegoat* is treated as a type picture of Satan. Adventists distinguish between the goat that was sacrificed on the Day of Atonement (Lv. 16), which typifies Christ, and the goat which was sent into the wilderness 'to Azazel' (Lv. 16:8,10). In this second goat they see Satan, who is to be punished as the instigator of all the sins in the world. One can only say that this is far from obvious, since the goat is not identified with Azazel – a possible name for a demon or for Satan. There is still something to be said for the old translation of 'scapegoat' or 'for removal'. If so, the two goats together represent two aspects of the atonement: one sacrificial to gain entrance into the Holy of Holies; the other to carry away our sins.

3. They regard *Michael the archangel* as a pre-incarnate title of Christ. The name means, 'Who is like God?' Theirs is a possible interpretation so long as one also accepts His full deity, as the Adventists do, and do not follow Jehovah's Witnesses, who also hold that Michael is Christ but believe that he was a created being.

These three points are quirks of interpretation, and it is surprising that Adventists make them part of their doctrinal system.

4. Mrs Ellen White has been accused of holding that Christ took a sinful human nature. This is a misunderstanding of her teaching that Christ assumed the liabilities of fallen humanity, such as the process of growing old, or tiredness and the capacity to die, together with being open to genuine temptation.

Note

About books
The Adventists have published a reasoned account of their beliefs in a substantial book of 720 pages, *Questions on Doctrine* (1957). An assessment that is critical and yet more favourable than some Christian works is Walter R. Martin, *The Truth about Seventh-Day Adventism* (Zondervan, and Marshall, Morgan and Scott, 1960). He was answered by another Christian writer, Norman F. Douty, in *Another Look at Seventh-Day Adventism* (Baker, and Marshall, Morgan and Scott, 1962). It appears likely that Adventists vary in their emphasis and their desire to oppose orthodox Christians.

Appendix

The Christian belief in the Trinity

SINCE SO MANY of these modern faiths reject the Christian doctrine of the Trinity, it is worth summarizing the reasons for this belief. It was not invented as an addition to the simple ideas of the Bible; but during the first three or four centuries AD the church was being continually bombarded by views of God that were based on one or two texts only. In the face of this, serious Christian thinkers were concerned to draw together all the relevant teachings of the Bible, and to crystallize them into formulae that would be a guide in interpreting individual texts. They did with the Bible what the scientist does when he formulates his laws from all the facts around him, and not simply from a few. Even when Protestants and Roman Catholics and Eastern Orthodox parted company, they all agreed that these creeds and summaries were true statements of what the Bible teaches. In recent years the rejection of the authority of the Bible has resulted in a desire to rewrite the doctrines.

So, although the Bible does not formulate a doctrine of the Trinity, yet, if we gather all the facts about God that appear in the Bible as revelation, we are inevitably led to the Trinitarian belief.

The deity of the Father
This needs no proof texts, since it is taken for granted in the New Testament, and no-one denies it.

Jesus Christ was aware of a unique relationship with the Father. In Matthew 11:27 He says that He and the Father know each other in a way that no other person can experience. We note that the knowledge is reciprocal. Hence we are justified in seeing His claim to be the Son of God as an awareness of His divine nature. The Jews understood this, and accused Him of blasphemy because, being a man, He made Himself God (Jn. 10:33). Again, they tried to kill Him because He 'called God his Father, making himself equal with God' (Jn. 5:18). Jesus admits that the title *Elohim* (God or gods) is sometimes applied to God's deputy rulers, but says that the title, Son of God, is all the more applicable to Him, since He had been consecrated by the Father and sent into the world (Jn. 10:34–38).

It is important to notice how often Jesus Christ spoke of Himself as having been sent into the world (*e.g.* Jn. 5:23,24, 30; 8:18,26; 16:5; *cf.* Rom. 8:3). He had a previous life with the Father (Jn. 16:28; 17:5), and so did not have the first beginning of existence at birth, as we have.

Other uses of the title 'Son of God' are significant. In the temptation in the wilderness He did not dispute Satan's use of His title (Mt. 4:1–11). The point of Satan's 'if' was not to throw doubt on His divinity, but to try to make Him misuse His divine powers. It is the 'if' of argument, as in the text, 'If God be for us, who can be against us?' (Rom. 8:31, AV). When demons were forced to admit that He was the Son of God, He did not deny it, but forbad them to make it known (Mk. 3:11,12). He needed to prepare the minds of His disciples to reach the inevitable conclusion that He was more than mere man. To have gone round continually asserting His deity would have been too much for their minds to bear. What He aimed at was to draw out an ultimate response such as Peter made in Matthew 16:16, 'You are the Christ, the Son of the living God', although it was not until after His resurrection and the coming of the Spirit that the full significance of the title dawned on the disciples. We realize that there are passages in the Bible to which we can return and find a fuller significance in them after we have had a further revelation in Scripture.

It is important also to note that, while Jesus Christ is the unique Son of God (*e.g.* Jn. 1:18, *etc.*), we may *become* sons of God through faith in Him (Jn. 1:12).

Whatever weight we may attach to the title 'Son of God', there are some plain texts that certainly teach Christ's deity:

a. John 1:1. In spite of what Jehovah's Witnesses say, the Greek can only mean 'The Word was God', or 'What God was, the Word was.'

b. John 8:58. 'Before Abraham was, I am.' This extraordinary use of the present tense can only be because Christ was claiming to have the name Jehovah (Ex. 3:14). The Jehovah's Witness *New World Translation* excels itself in evasion by translating, 'Before Abraham came into existence, I have been', an impossible rendering of the present tense.

c. John 20:28. Christ accepts Thomas's worship of Him as 'My Lord and my God'. This cannot be simply a pious exclamation, since no Jew would thus take God's name in vain.

d. Philippians 2:6. The technical term, *form* of God, can only mean *having the nature of God*, or *all that constitutes God as God*. If we deny this meaning, we must also deny the manhood of Christ, since exactly the same Greek word is used in verse 7 of His taking the *form* of a servant.

e. Hebrews 1:8. Christ is here distinguished from angels and men by being given the title *God*.

f. Matthew 1:23; Luke 1:35. His conception through the action of the Holy Spirit demonstrated that He was Son of God and God with us.

These are a few clear texts, but Christ's deity underlies the whole New Testament. Thus His promise to be with all His people all the time could be fulfilled only if He is God (Mt. 28:20). He is identified with Jehovah (Yahweh) in John 12:40,41, which says that the vision of Jehovah that Isaiah saw in Isaiah 6 was a vision of Christ. Similarly Revelation

2:23 applies to Christ the claims of Jeremiah 17:9, 10, that only Jehovah can search the heart of man.

If Christ is God, He cannot be a created being. He and the Father must be eternal, as is also the Holy Spirit. Thus the title *Son* is pictorial rather than genetic, and includes the concept of the One who is heir of all things (Col. 1:15–20). Note that Christ remembered His pre-incarnation existence with His Father (Jn. 17:5).

The deity of the Holy Spirit

To lie to the Holy Spirit is to lie to God (Acts 5:3, 4). The linking of the Spirit with the Lord Jesus and the Father in such places as 1 Corinthians 12:4–6 and 2 Corinthians 13:14 would be near blasphemy if He were not Himself God. The Holy Spirit is also personal. Thus He wills (Acts 13:2; 1 Cor. 12:11); He understands (Rom. 8:27); He may be grieved (Eph. 4:30). Such terms would be meaningless if applied to an impersonal influence or power.

The distinction between the Three

At the baptism of Jesus Christ, He was in the Jordan, the Father's voice was heard from heaven and the Holy Spirit descended on Him (Mk. 1:9–11). Christ on earth prayed to the Father, and promised that the Father would send the Holy Spirit (Jn. 14:26).

The unity of the Three

The presence of One means the presence of all. The Spirit of God in the heart means Christ in the heart (Rom. 8:9–11). There is a wonderful sequence in John 14:16, 18, 23, where the coming of the Spirit is the coming of Christ Himself, and also is the coming of the Father to dwell with the believer.

Conclusion

How can these facts be brought together? Not by postulating three Gods, since the Bible is emphatically monotheistic (*e.g.* Jas. 2:19). Not as a single God playing three parts at different times. The only summary that meets all the scriptural statements is *three Persons in one God*. God is one, but this oneness is not a bare mathematical unity. It involves personal relationship. Even in ourselves we are aware of some shadow of this higher unity. We are one, and yet we are personal in our body and personal in our mind. My body is involved in all that my mind is, and my mind is involved in all that my body is, but there are certain things that my mind does and others that my body does. It is proper to say that I, as my body, eat my meals, and I, as my mind, travel abroad with my ideas. Similarly it is proper to say that the second Person of the Trinity, and not the Father, became man, and His incarnation did not break the Trinity.

Those who dismiss the doctrine of the Trinity as ridiculous should be reminded that three-dimensional space is a natural analogy of what we say about the Trinity. Space requires length, breadth and height. All three are equal in importance, and none is greater or less than the others. So we have three dimensions forming one space. For some purposes we treat them as one; for other purposes we separate them.